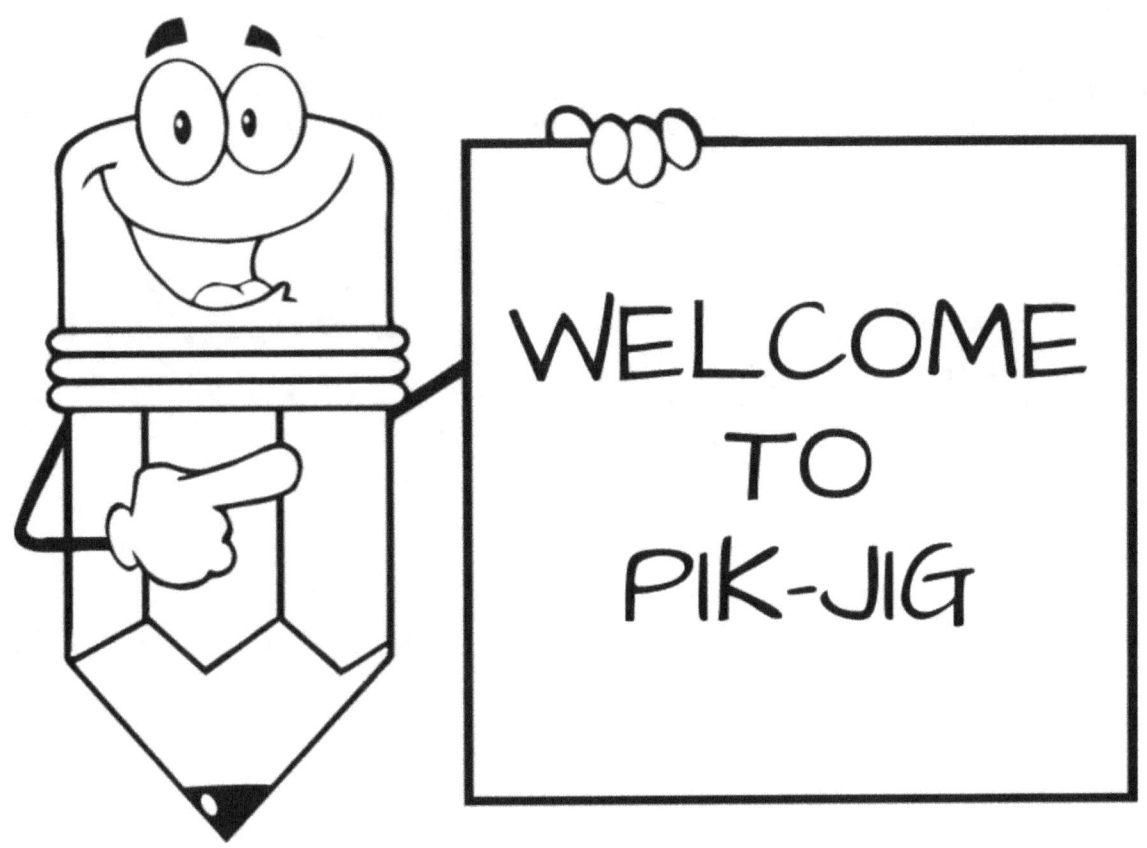

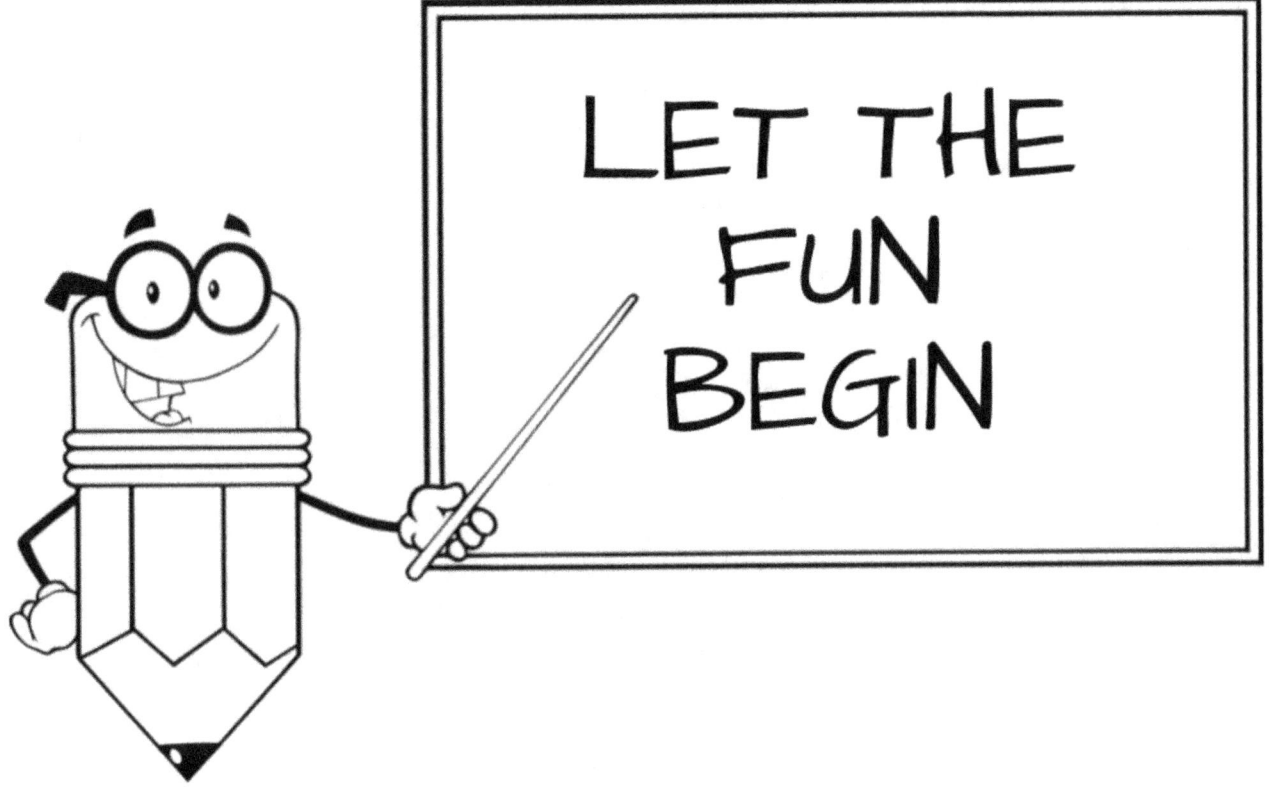

Copyright © 2024 by Pik-Jig

All rights reserved.

All rights reserved. No part of this publication may be reproduced, distributed, or transmitted in any form or by any means, including photocopying, recording, or other electronic or mechanical methods, without the prior written permission of the publisher, except in the case of brief quotations embodied in critical reviews and certain other noncommercial uses permitted by copyright law.

INSTRUCTIONS

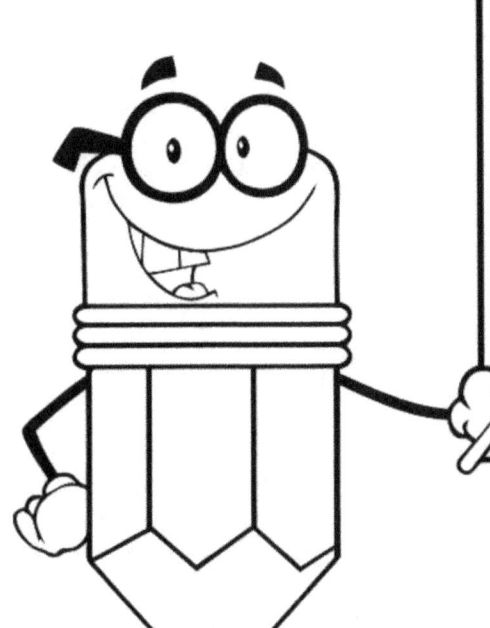

STEP ONE
PICK A SQUARE

STEP TWO
FIND THE SQUARE ON THE GRID BY
MATCHING THE COORDINATES

STEP THREE
DRAW WHAT YOU SEE AND WATCH
THE MAGIC UNFOLD

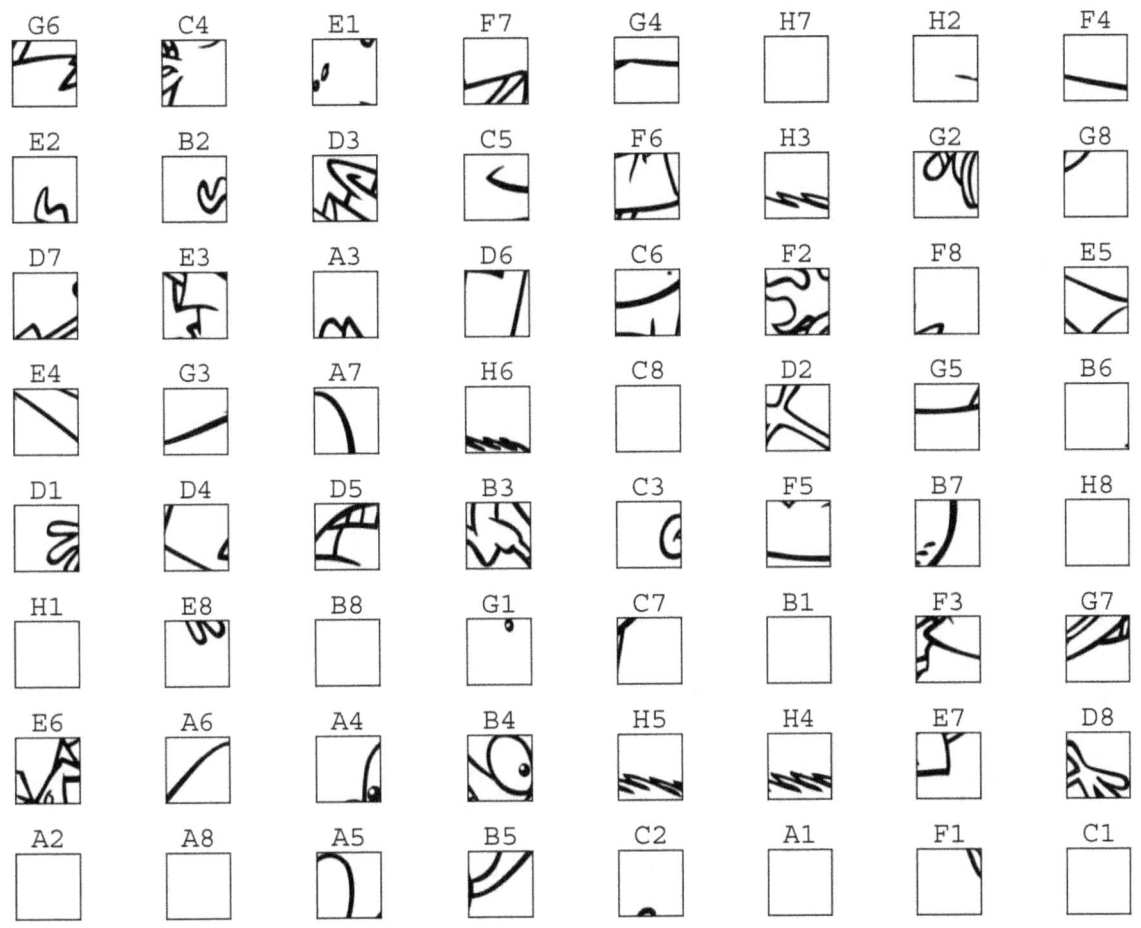
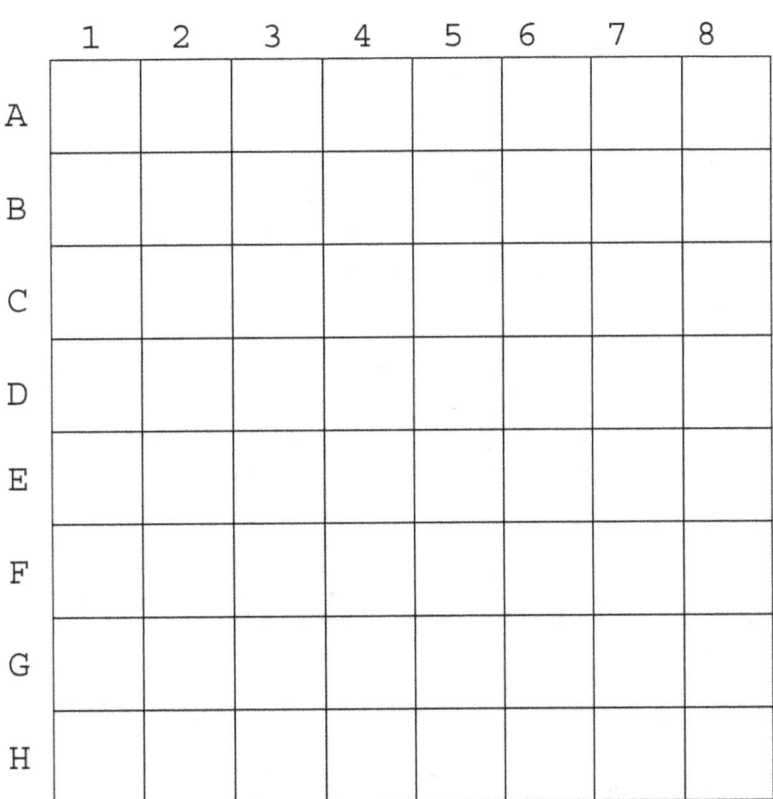

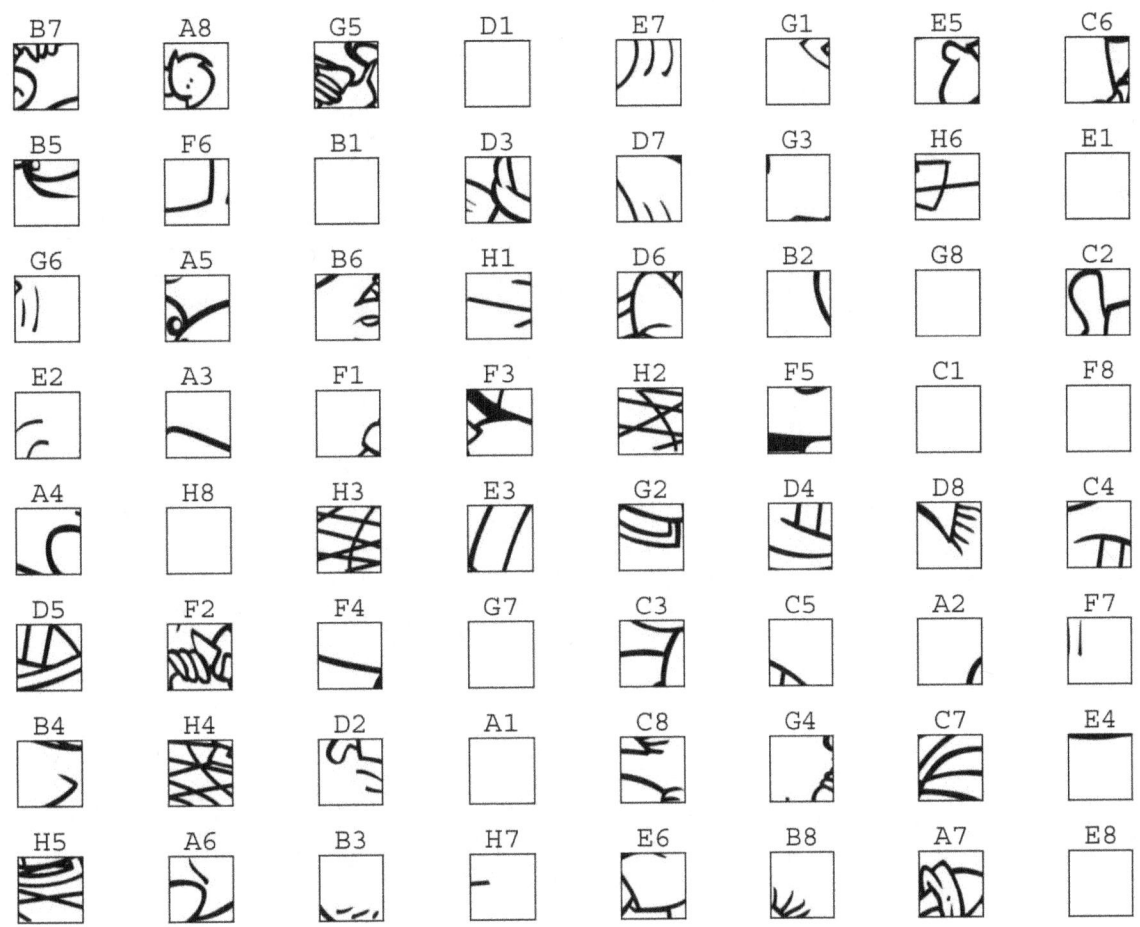
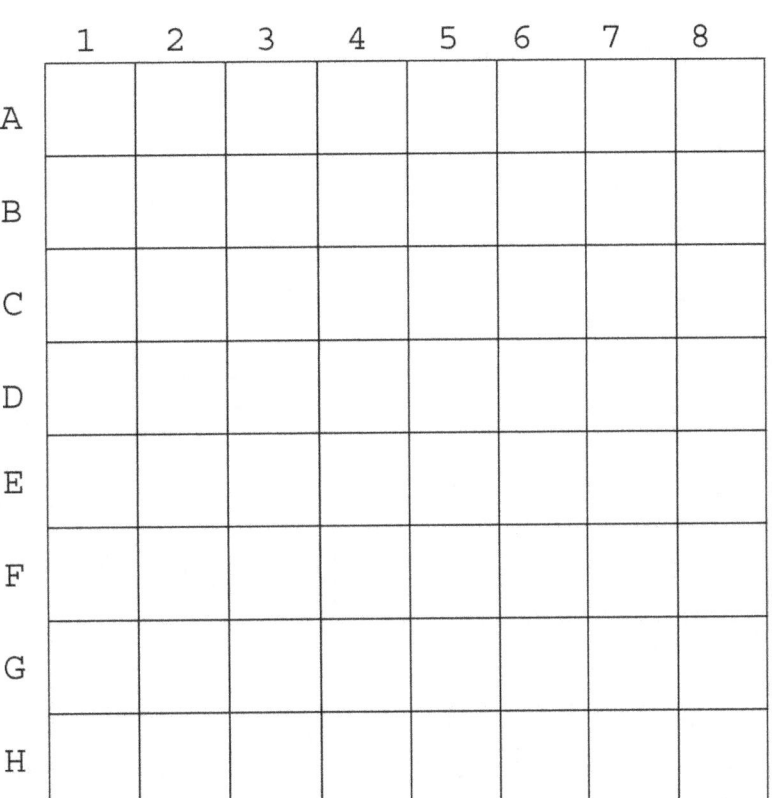

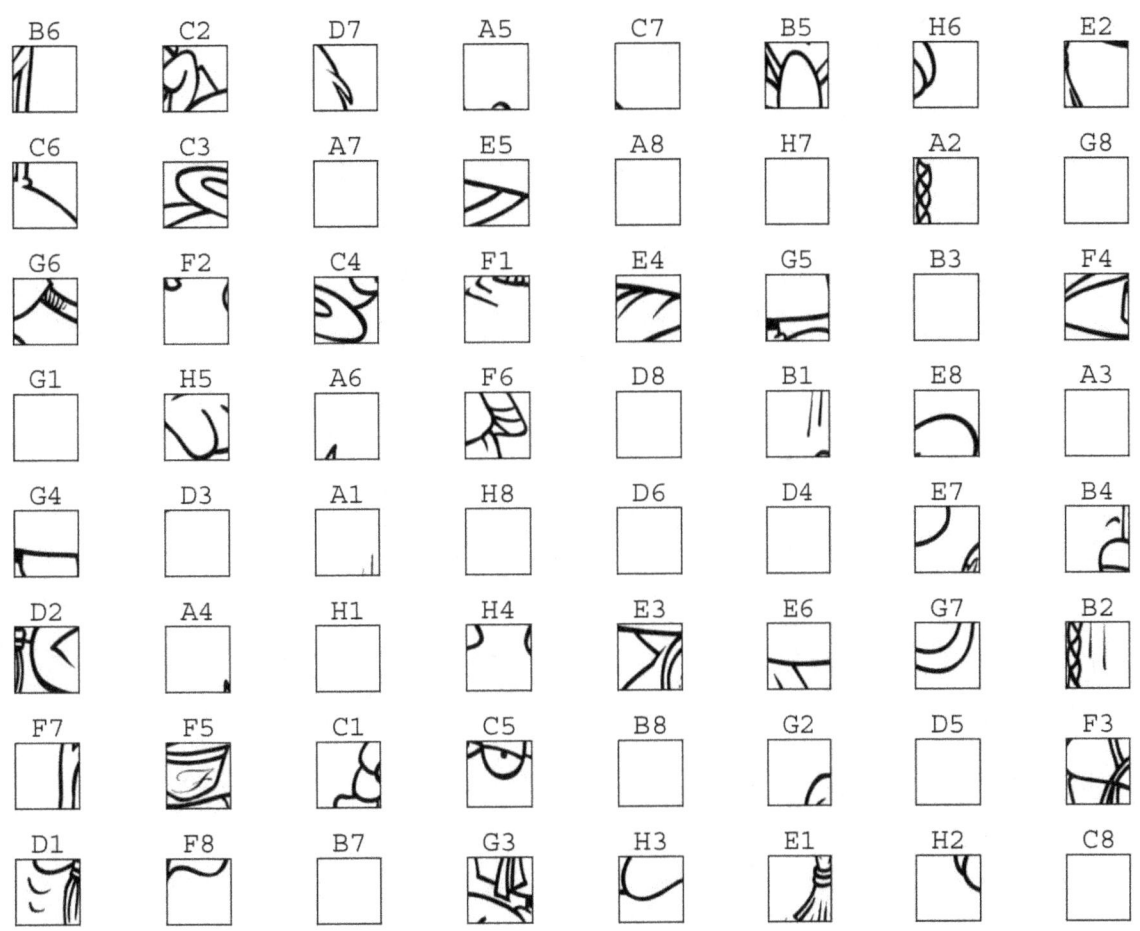
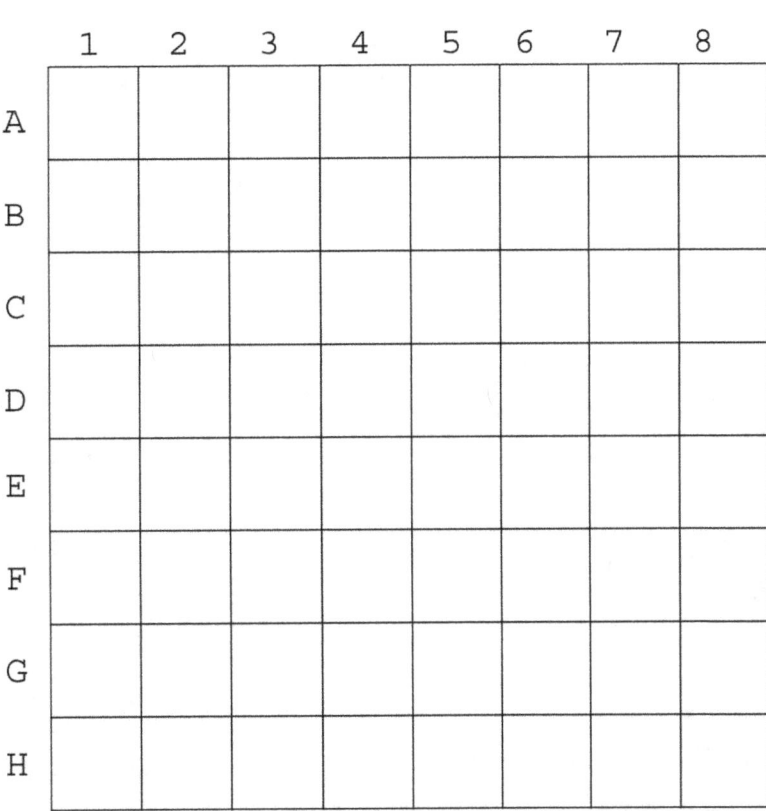

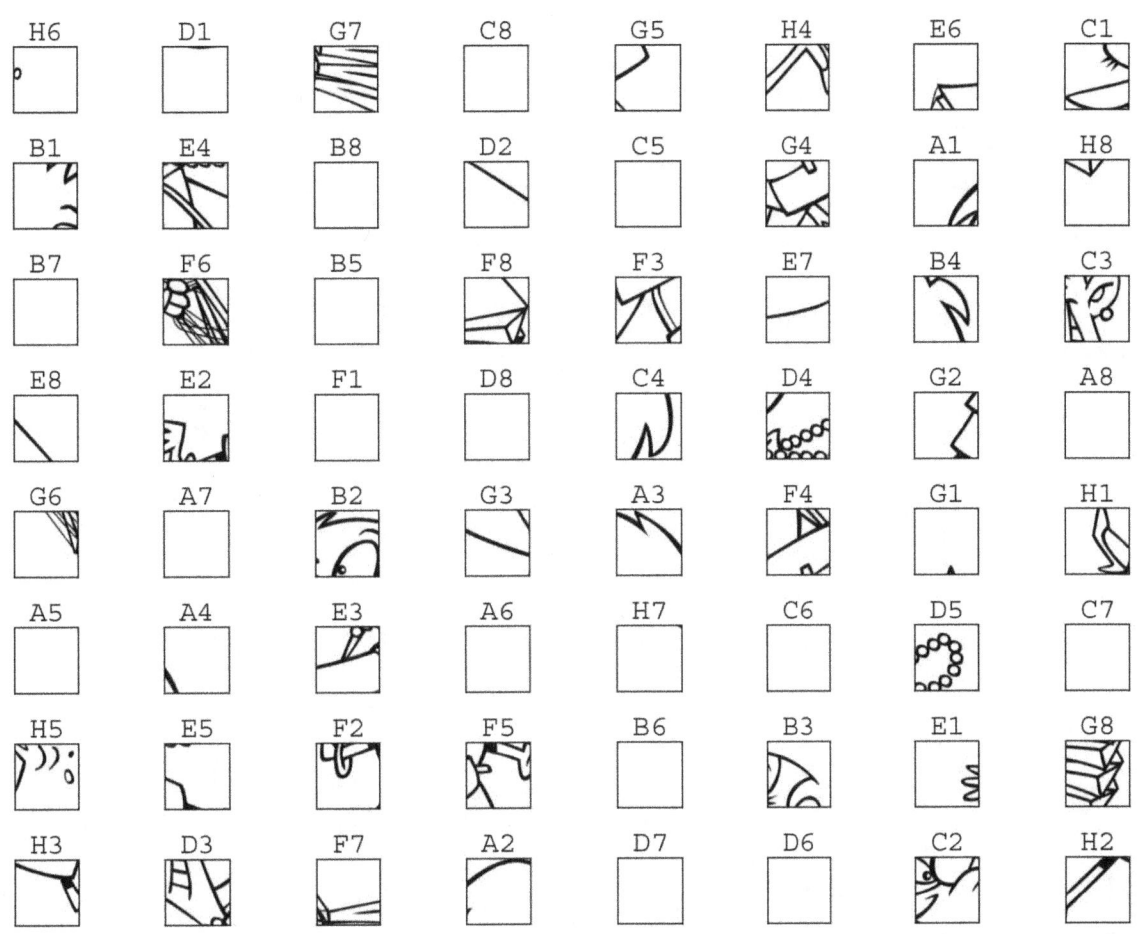
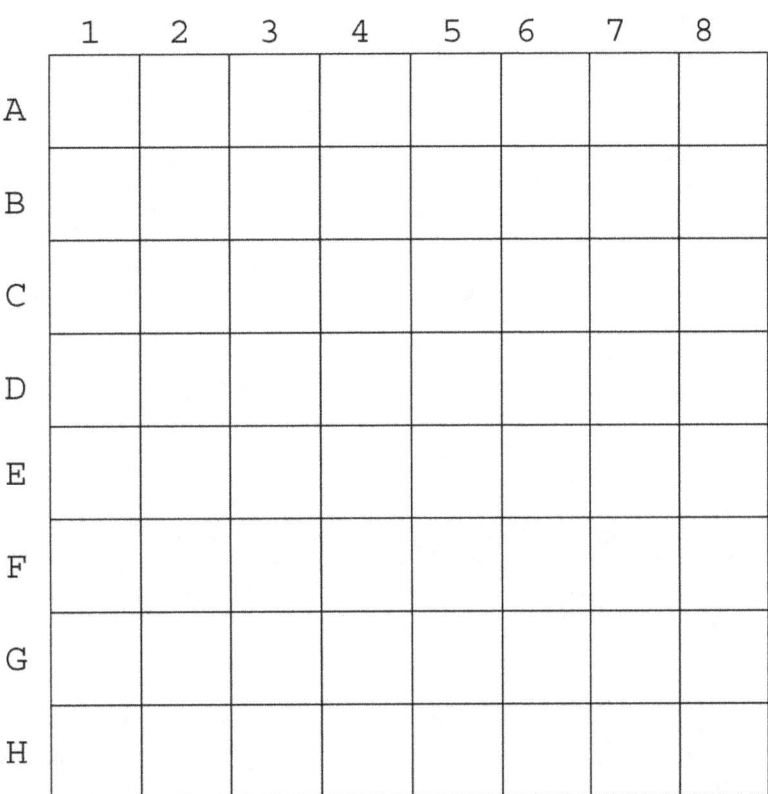

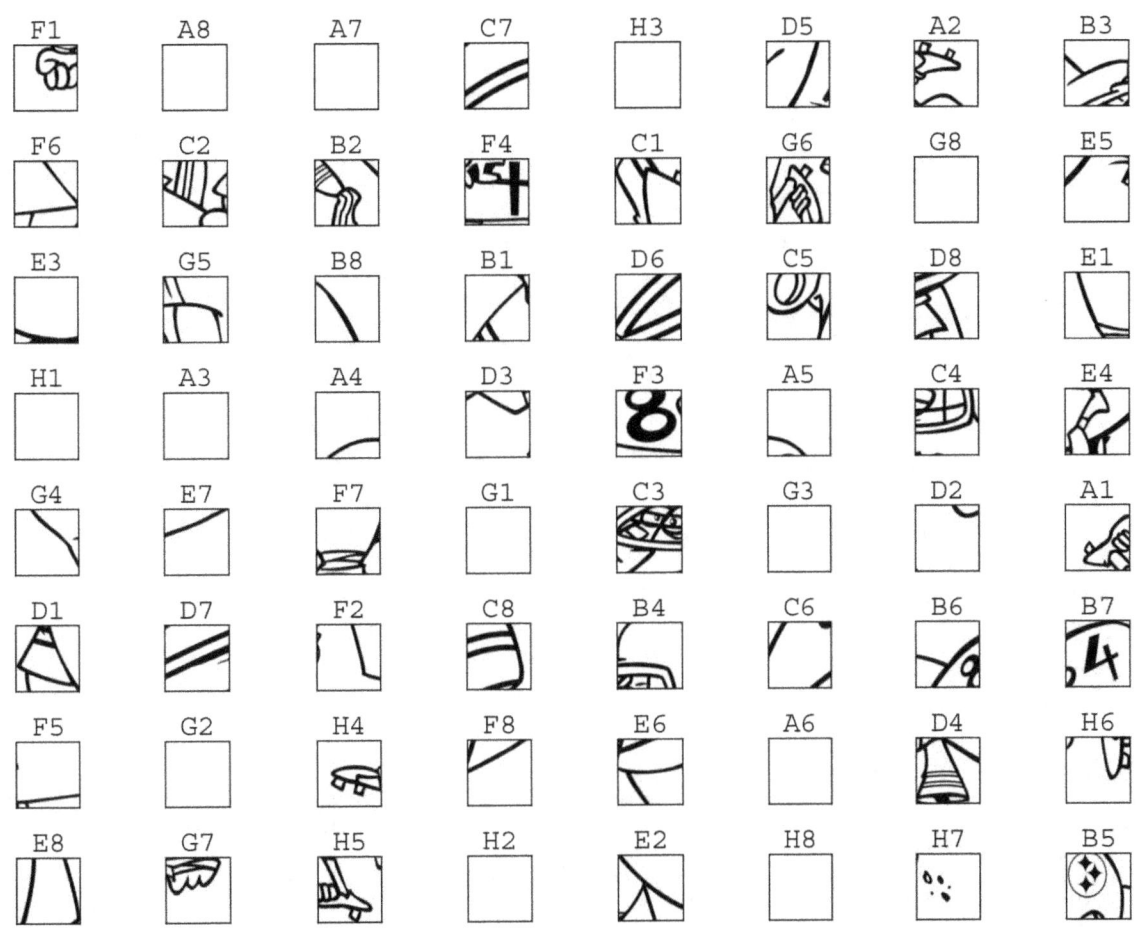
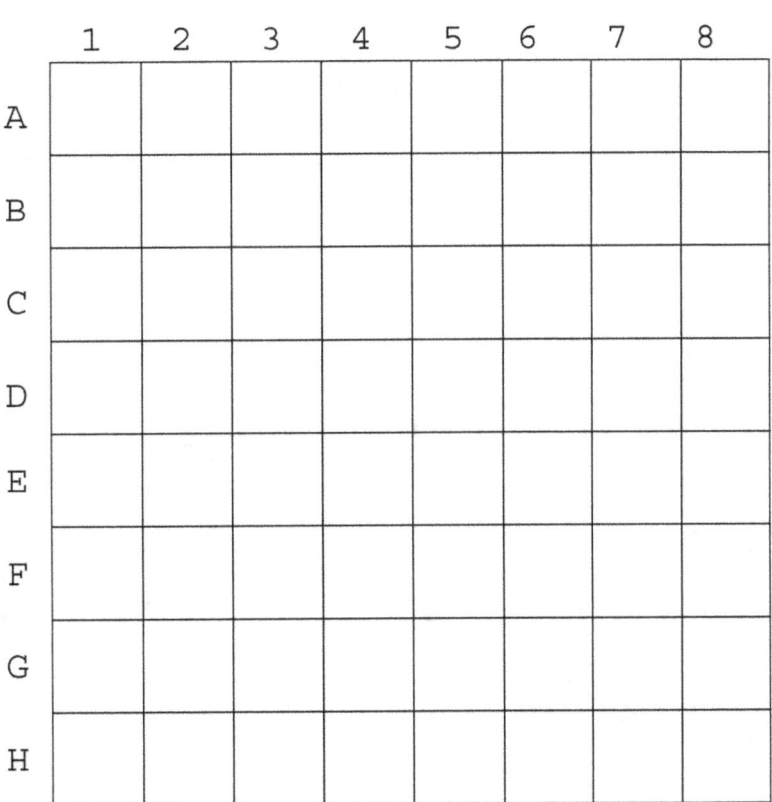

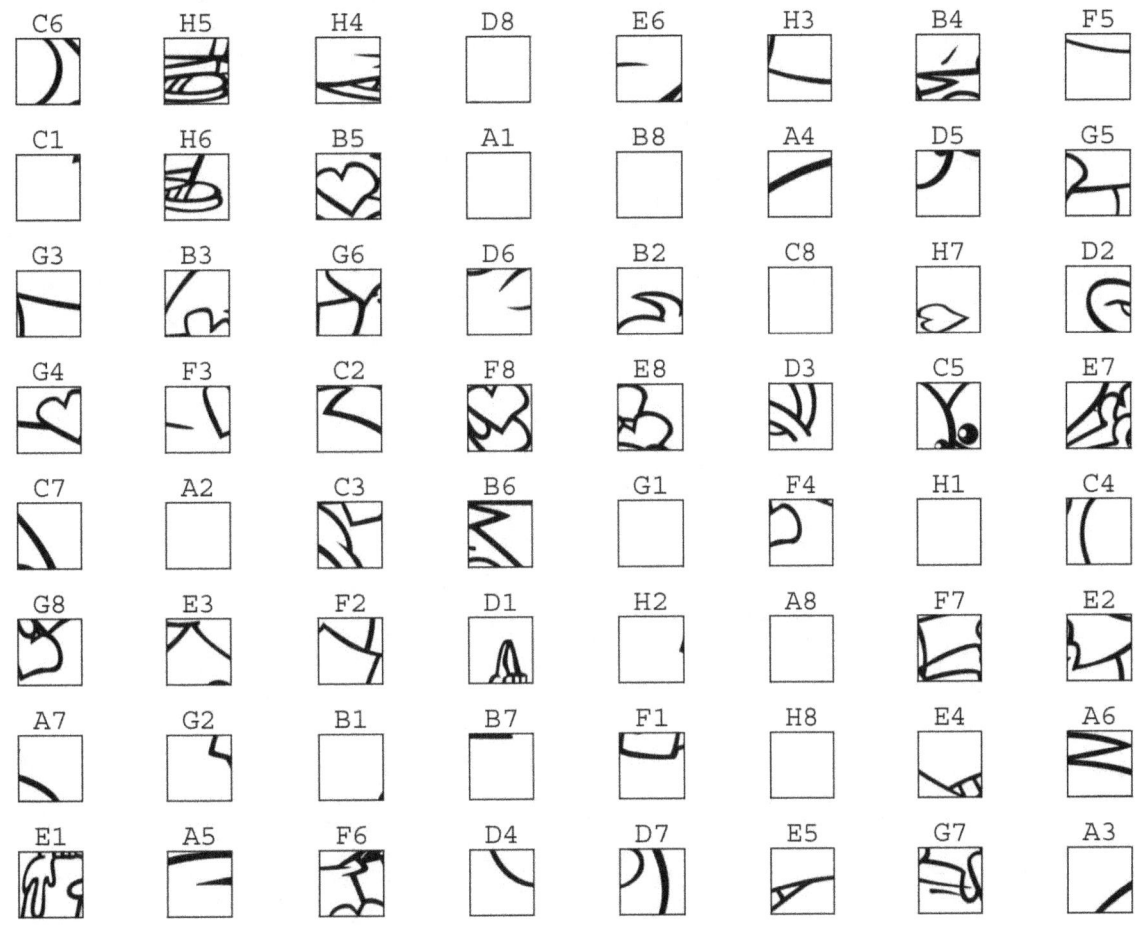
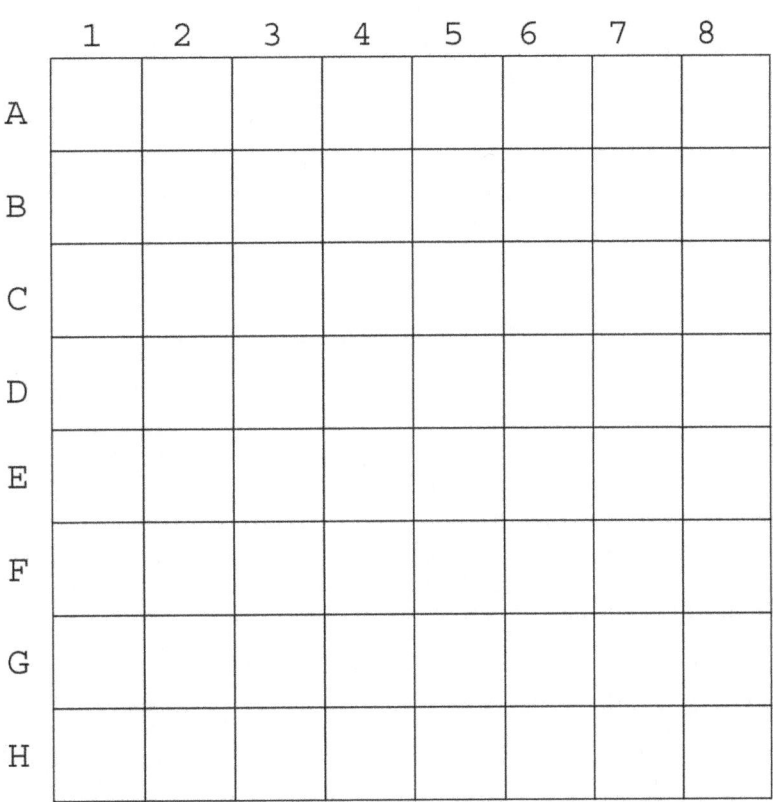

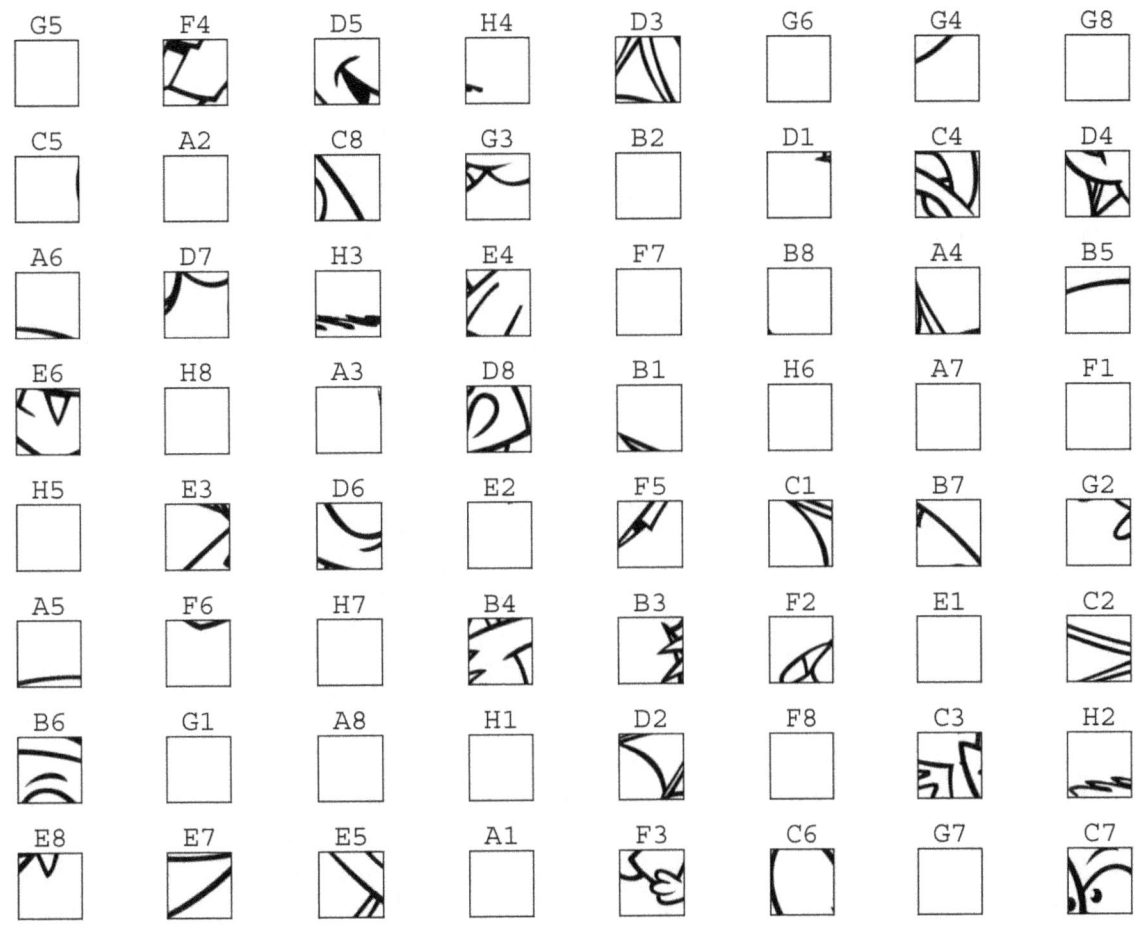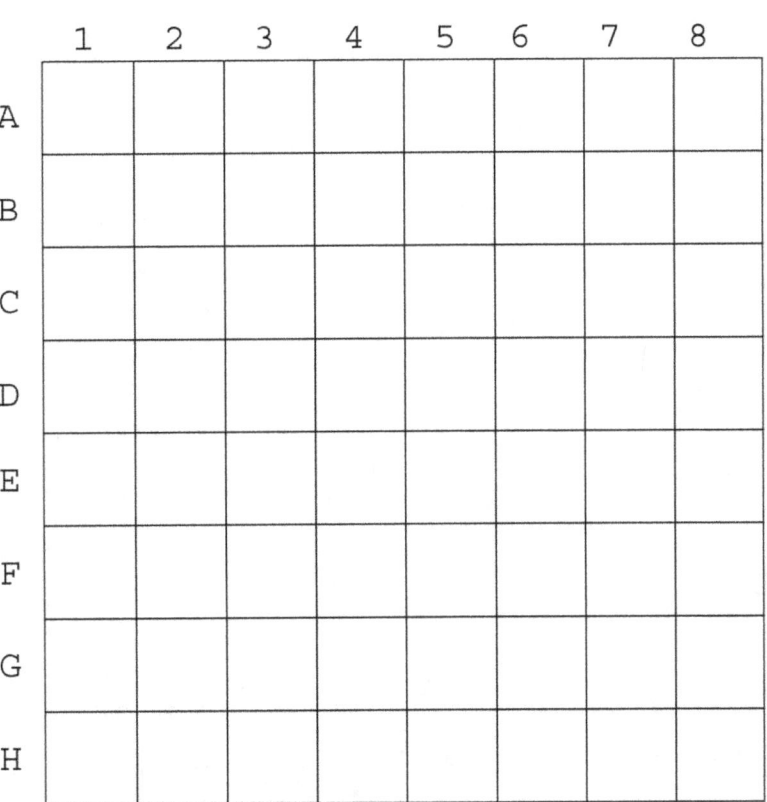

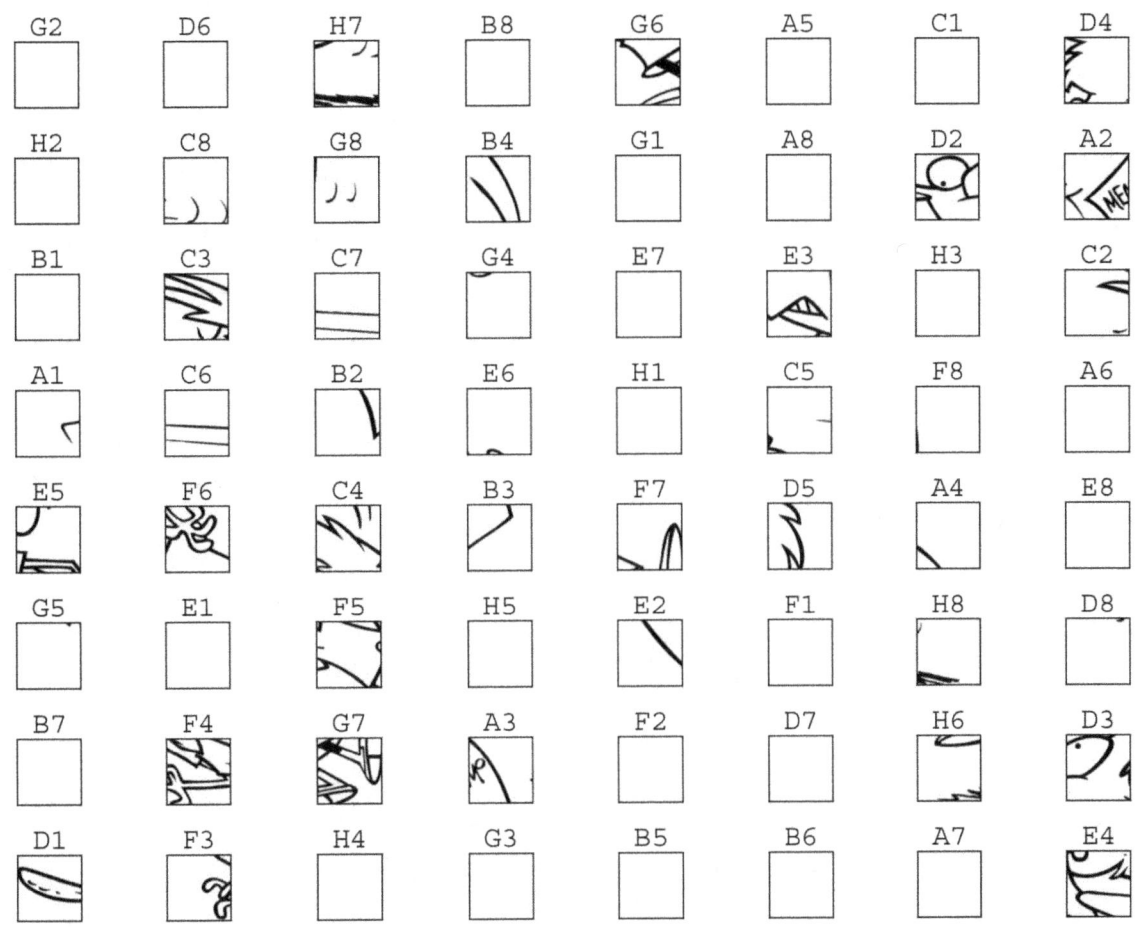
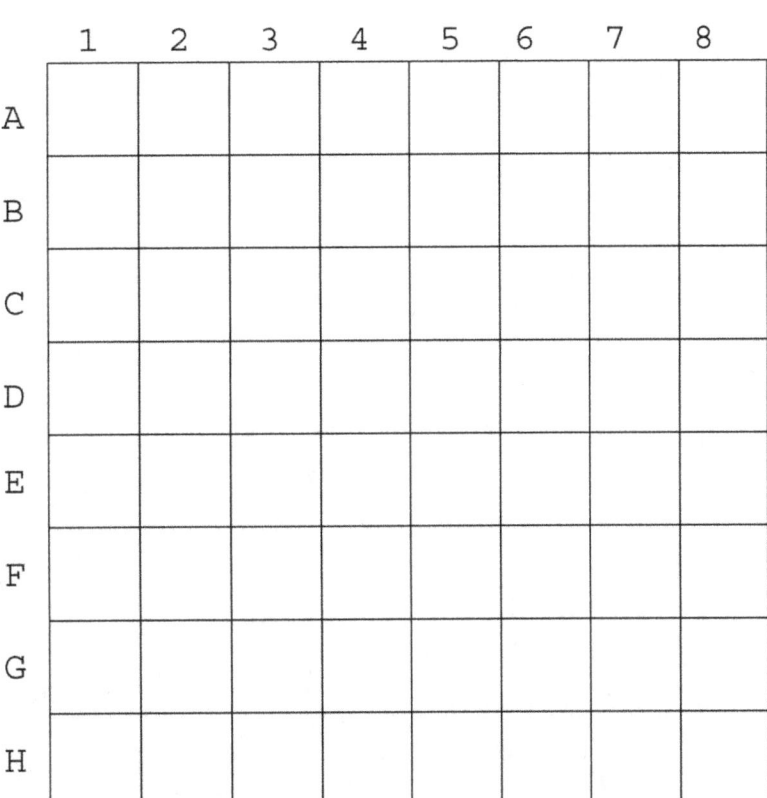

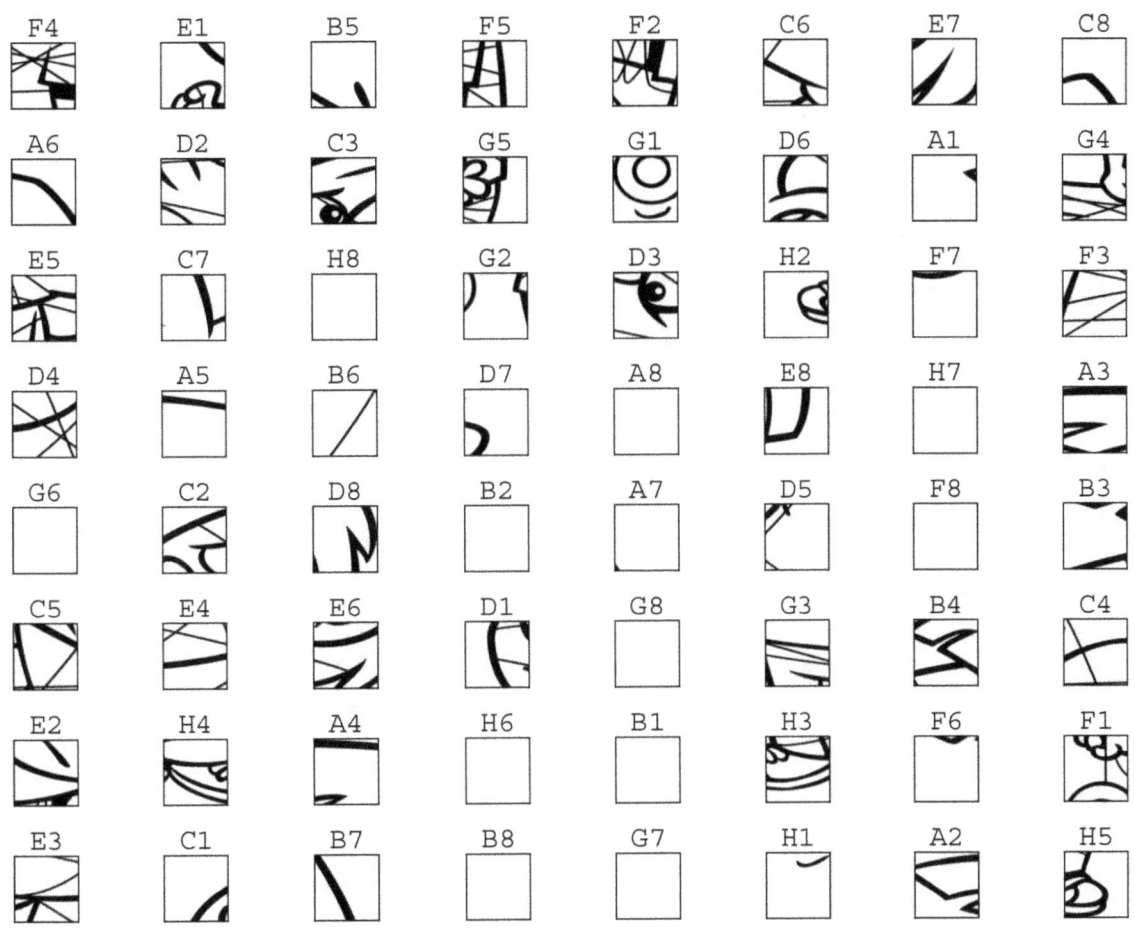
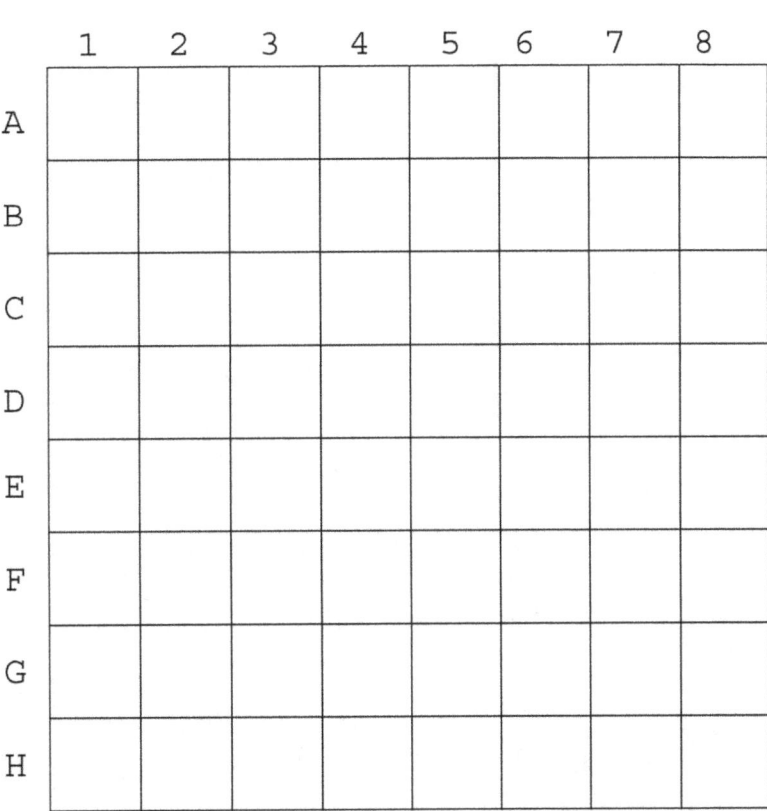

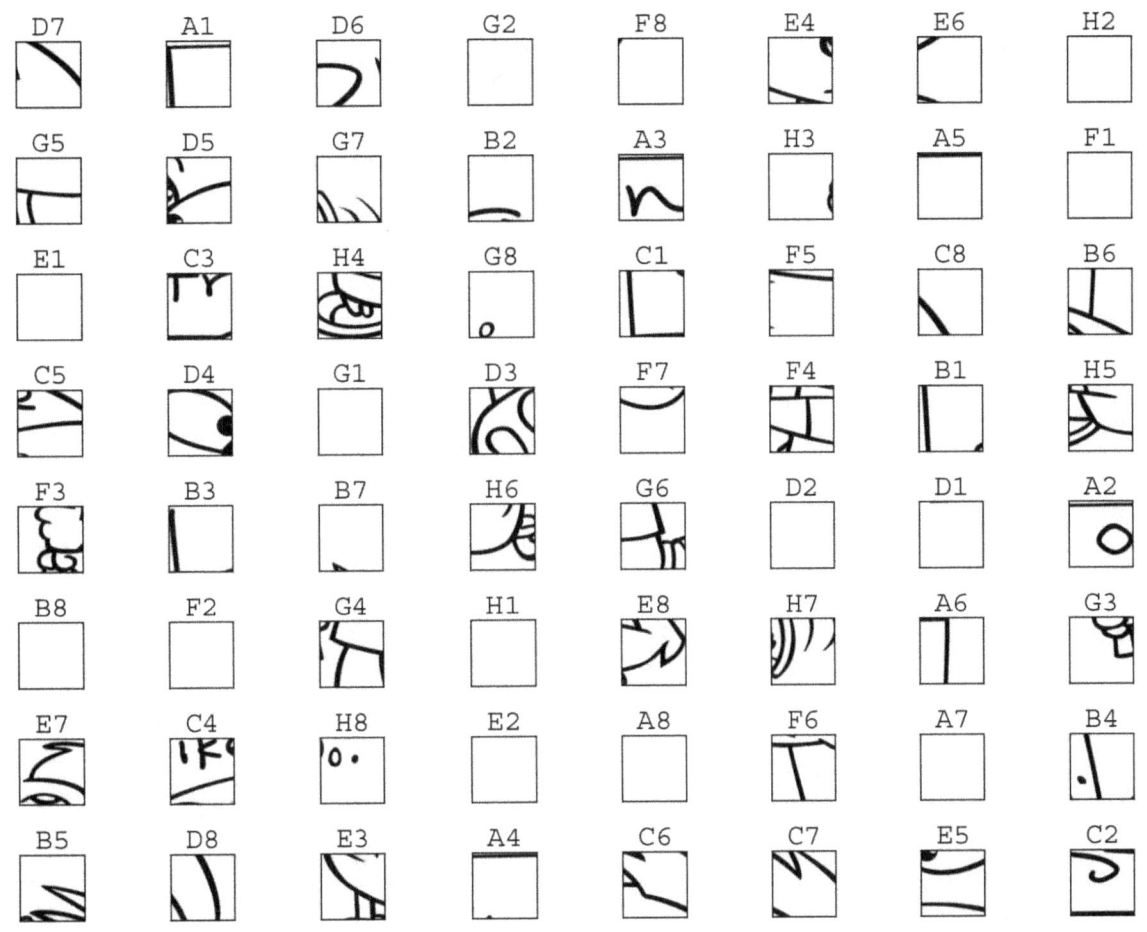
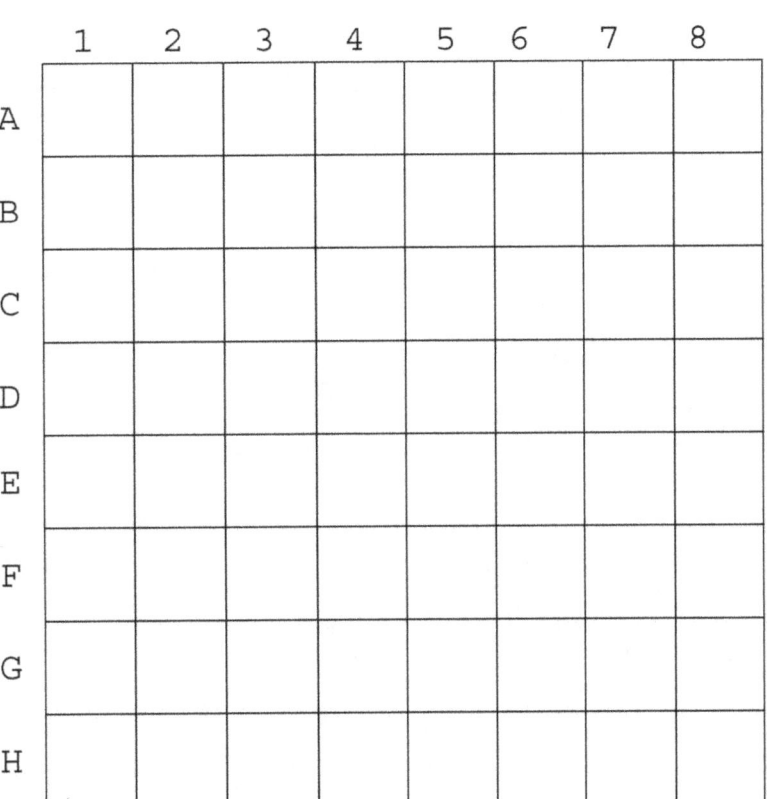

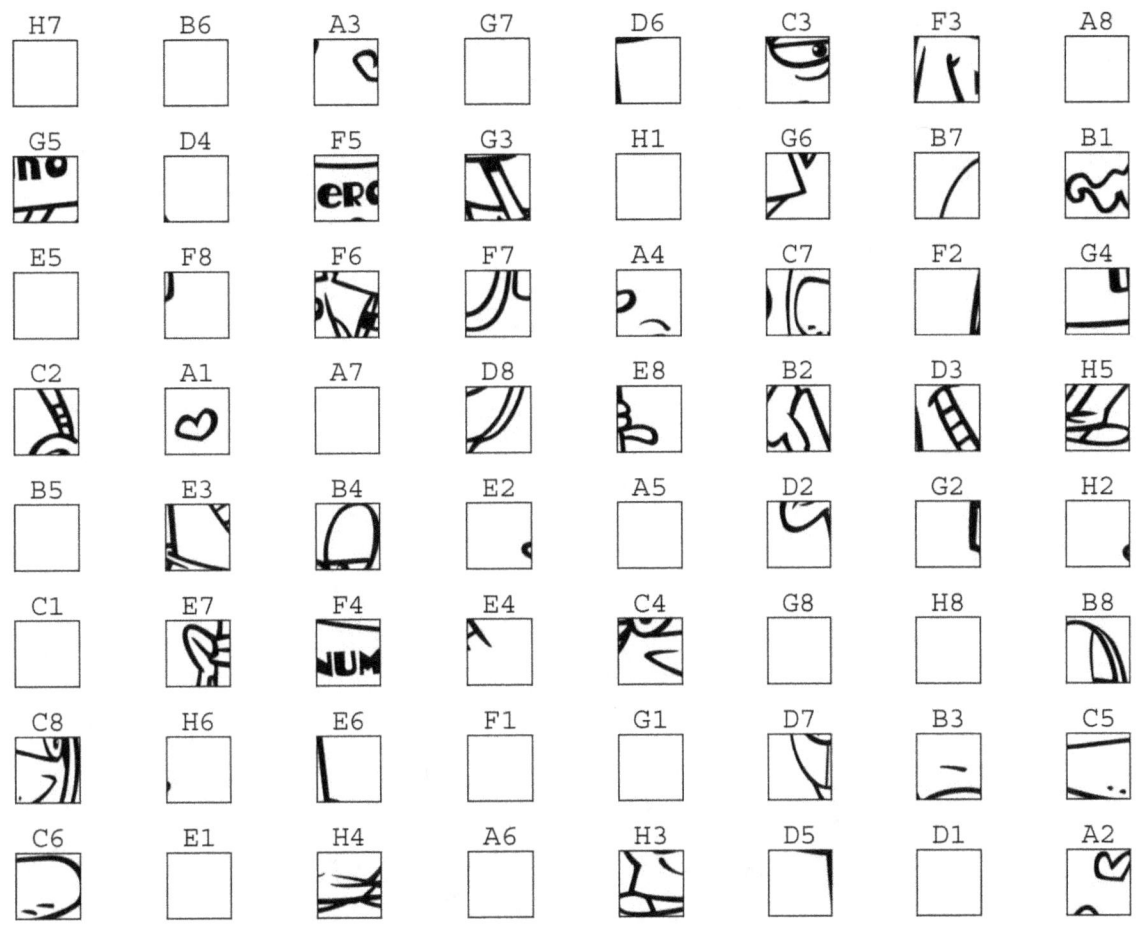
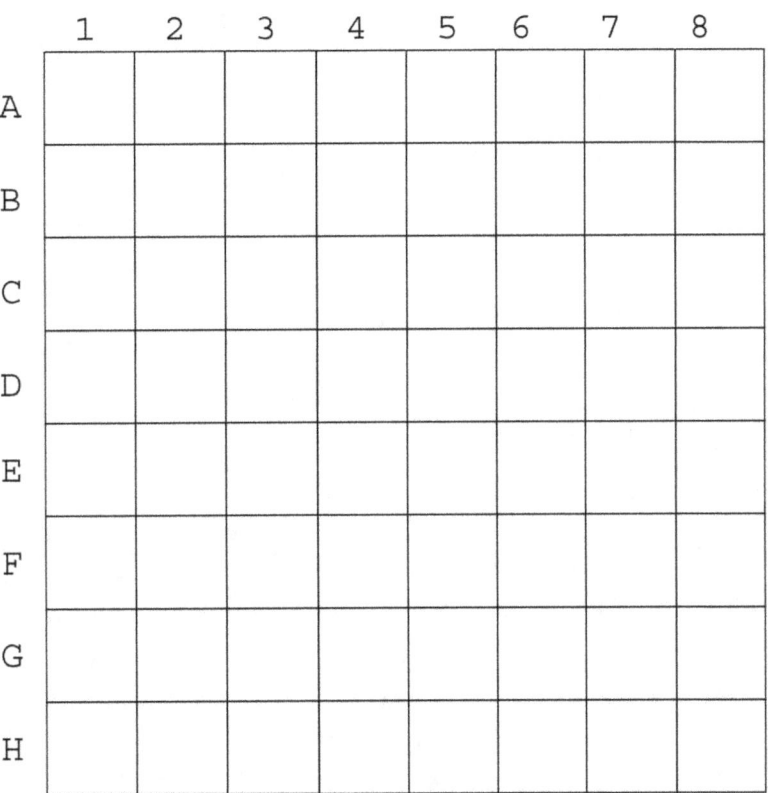

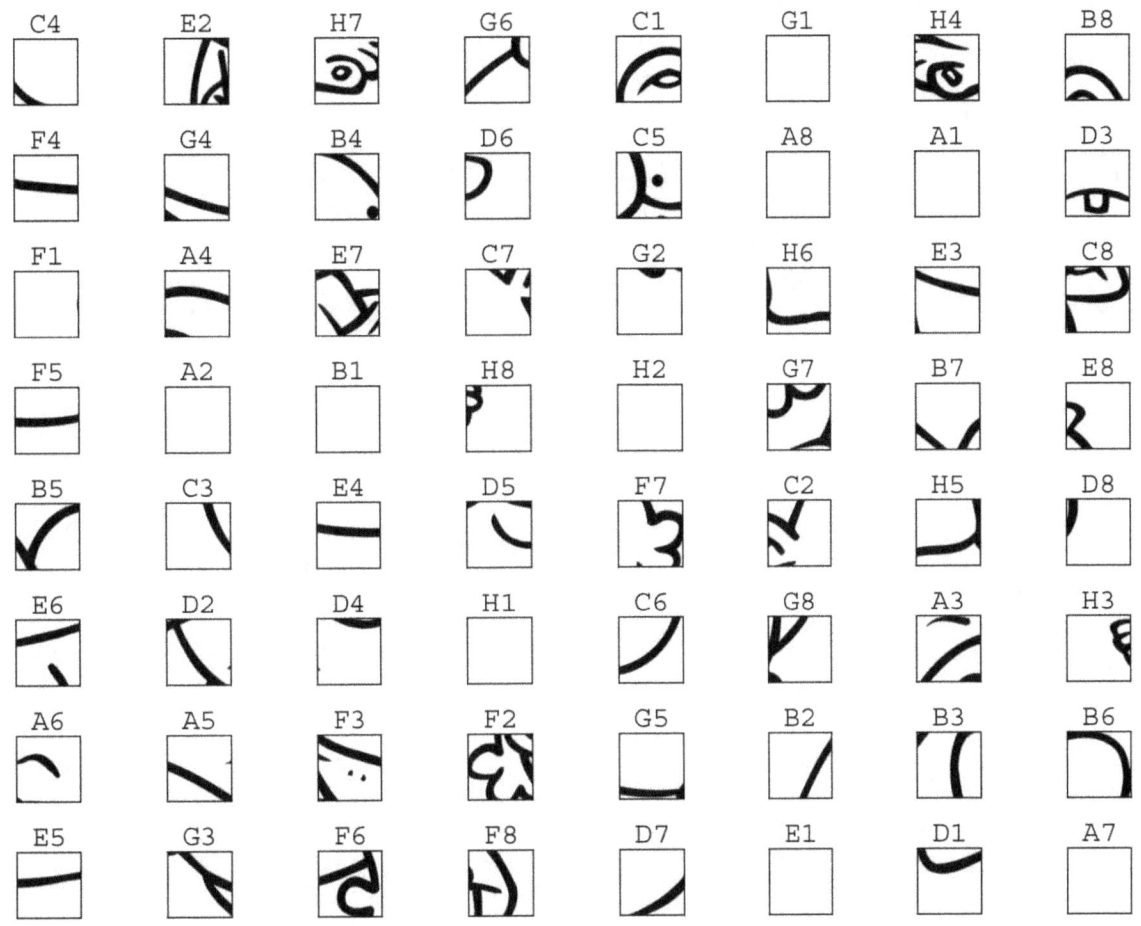
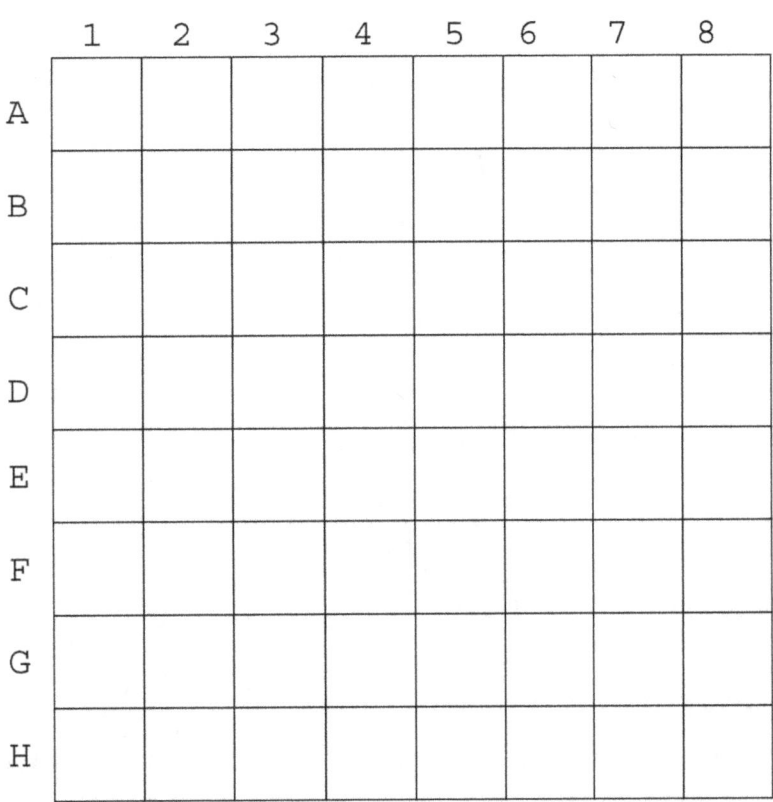

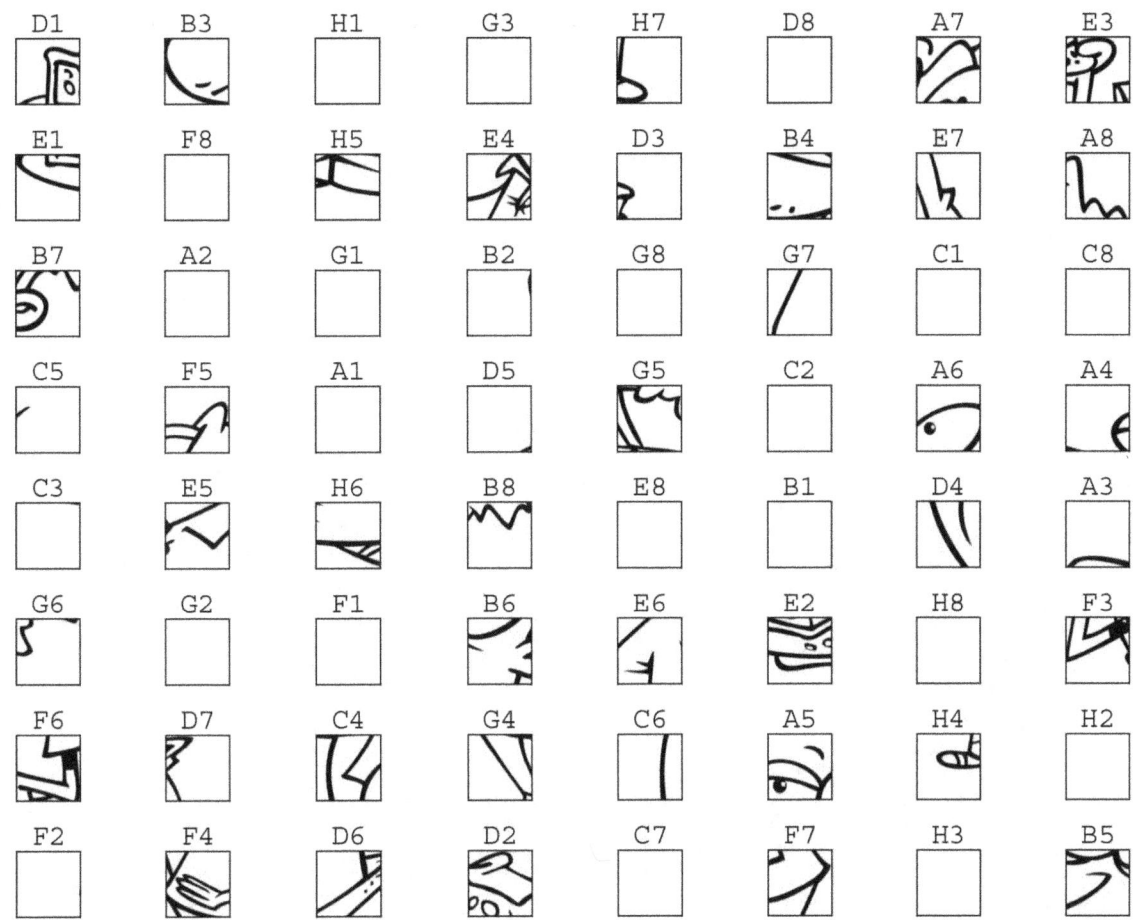
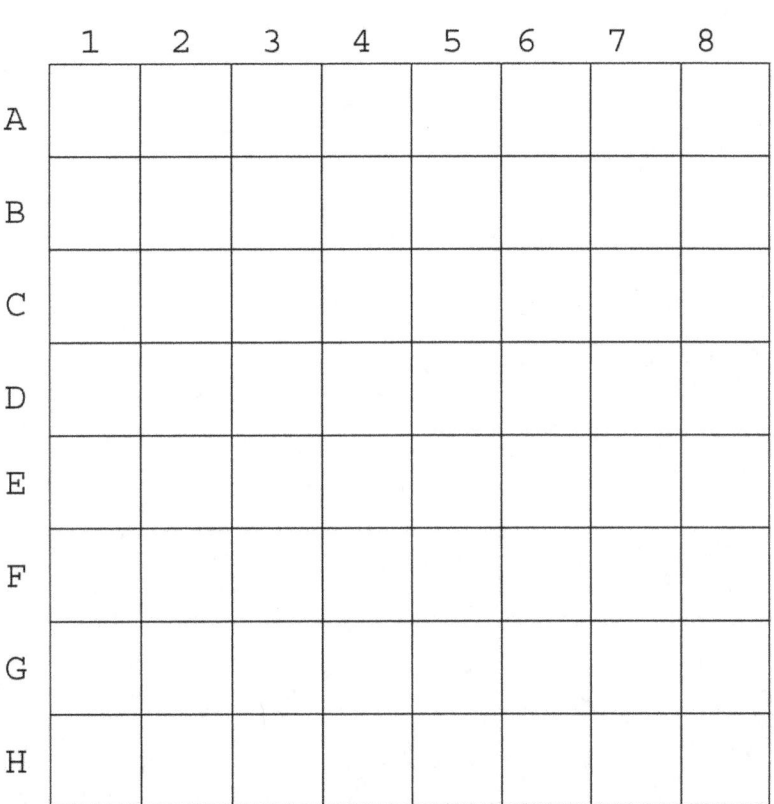

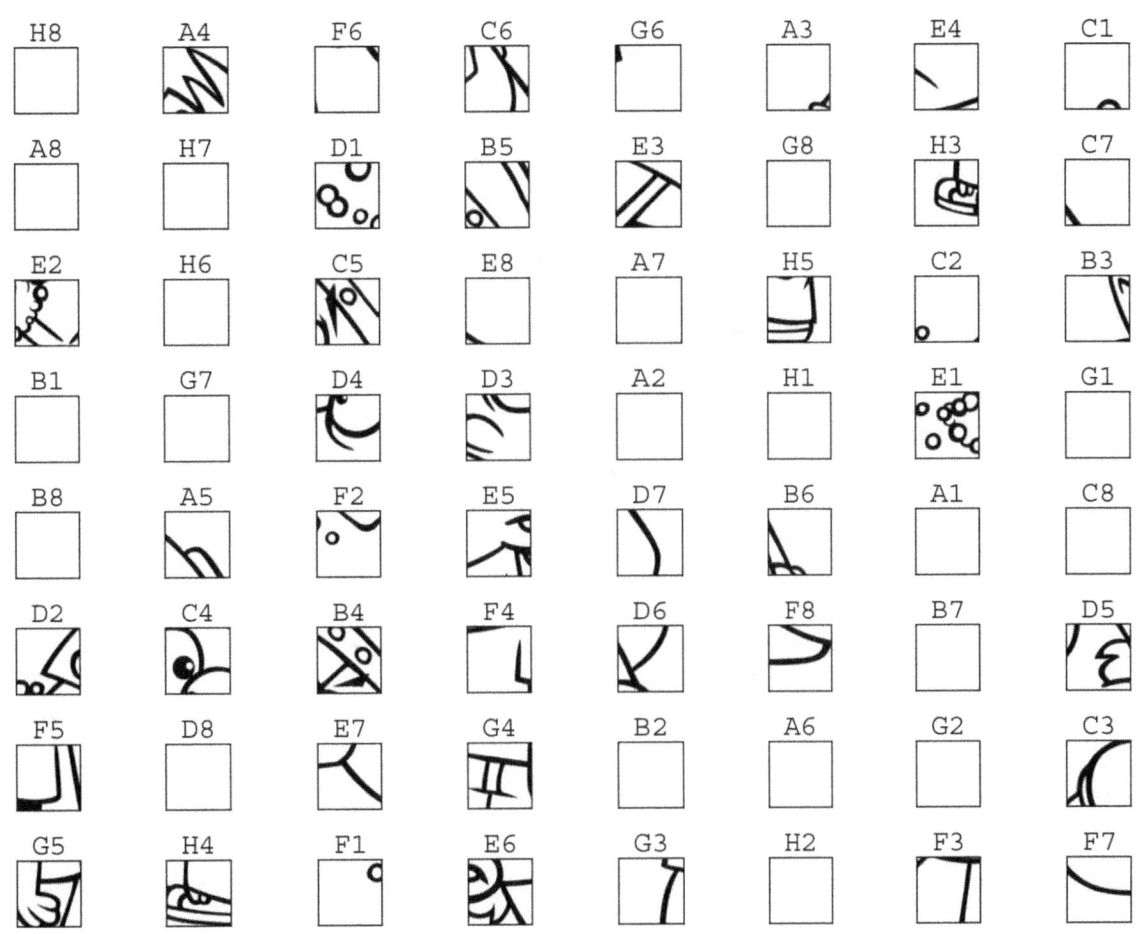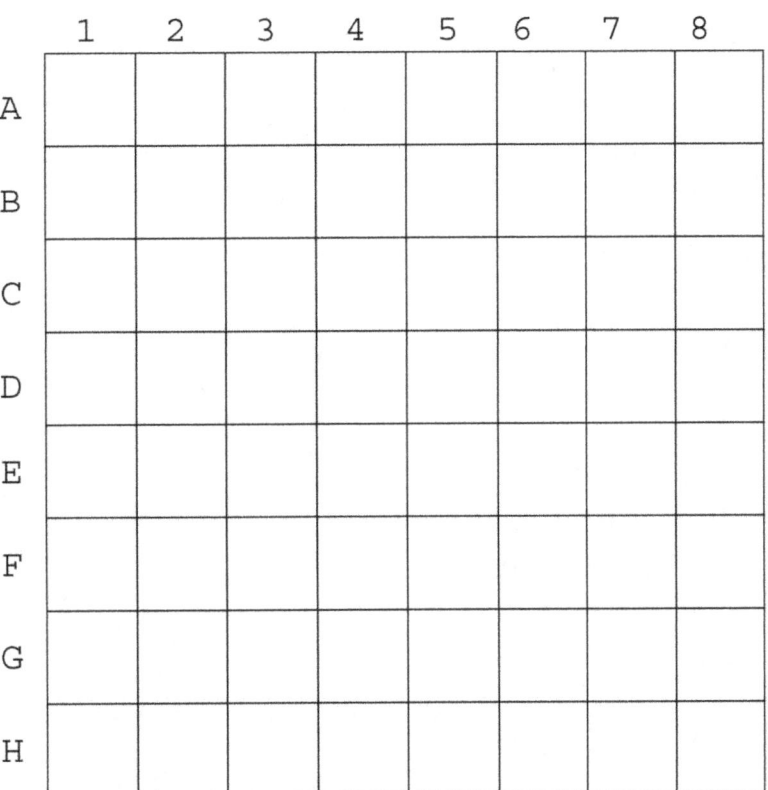

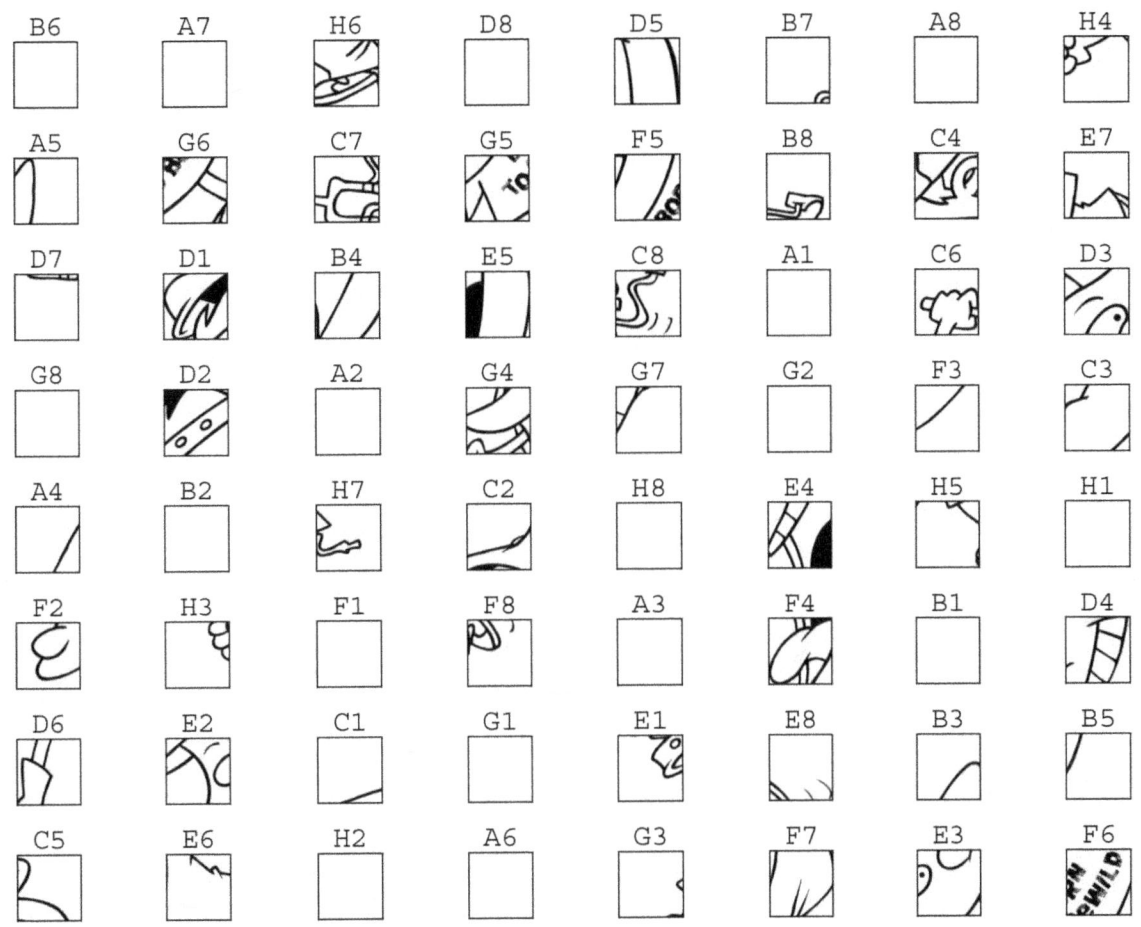
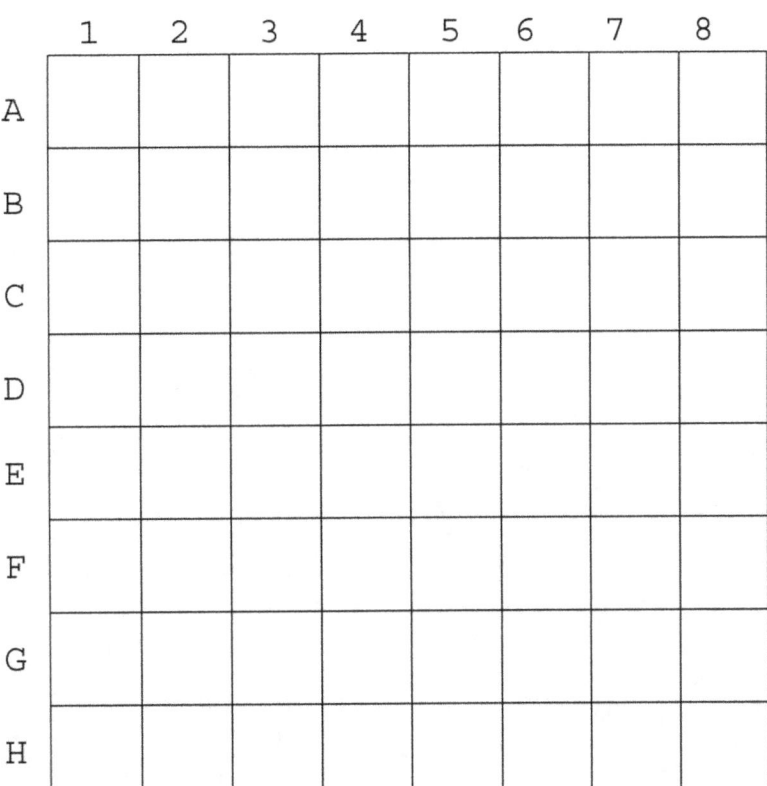

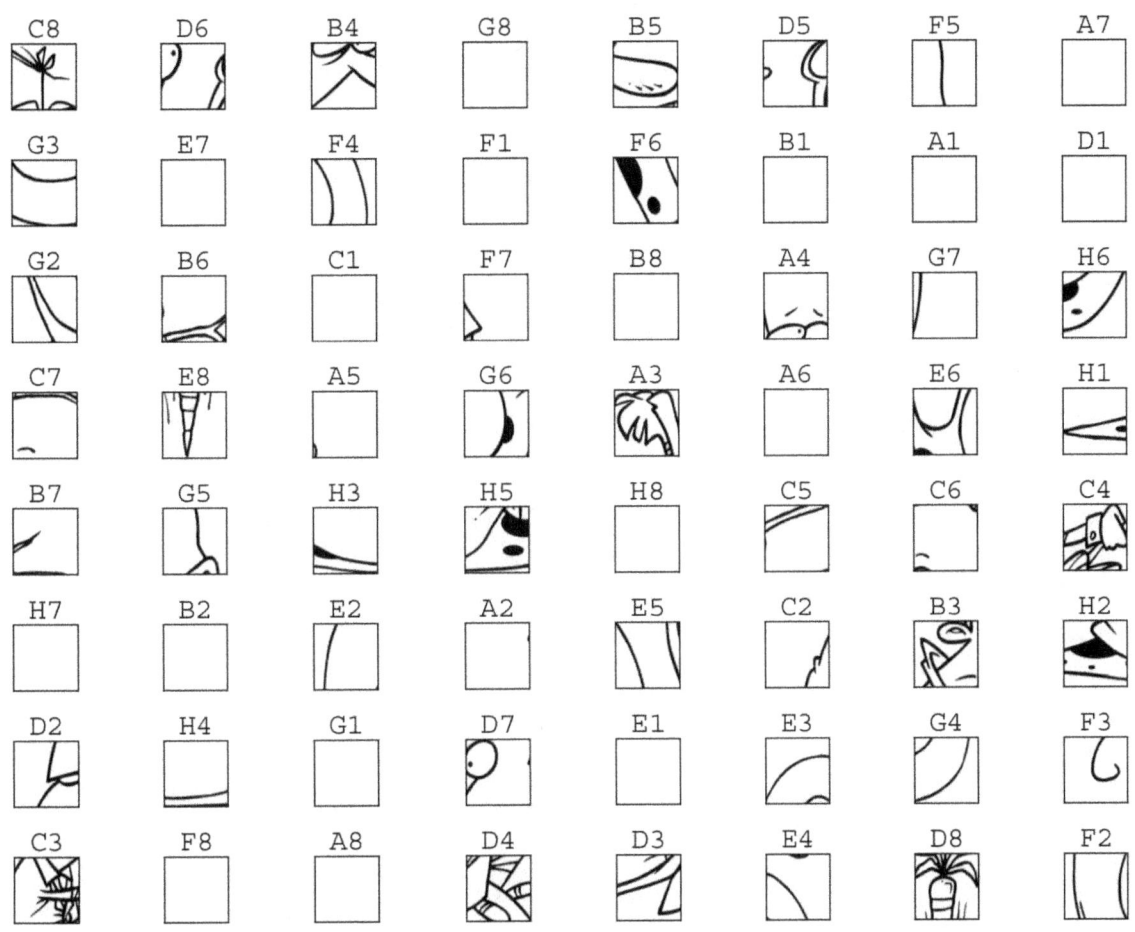
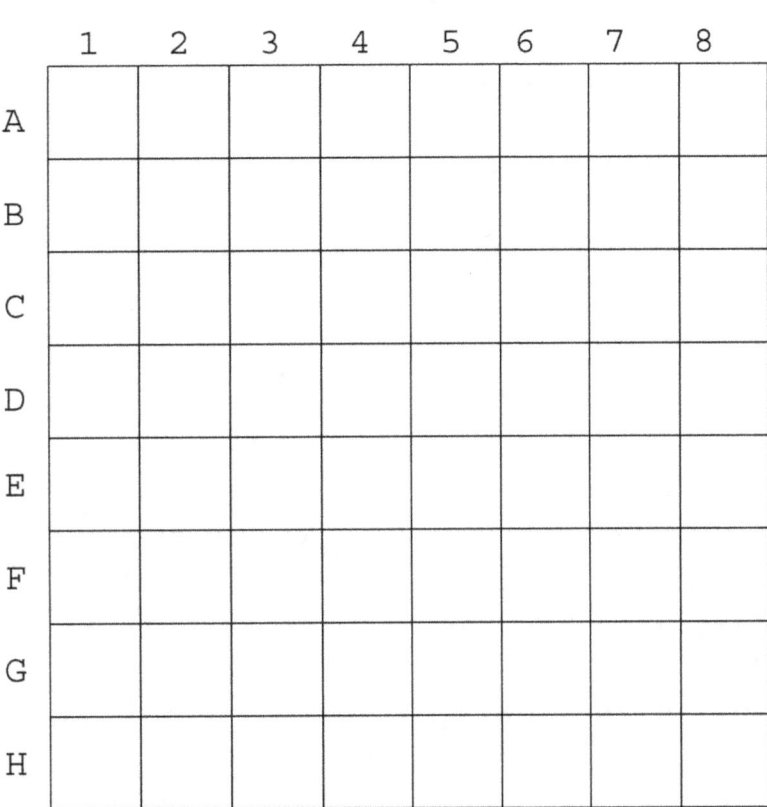

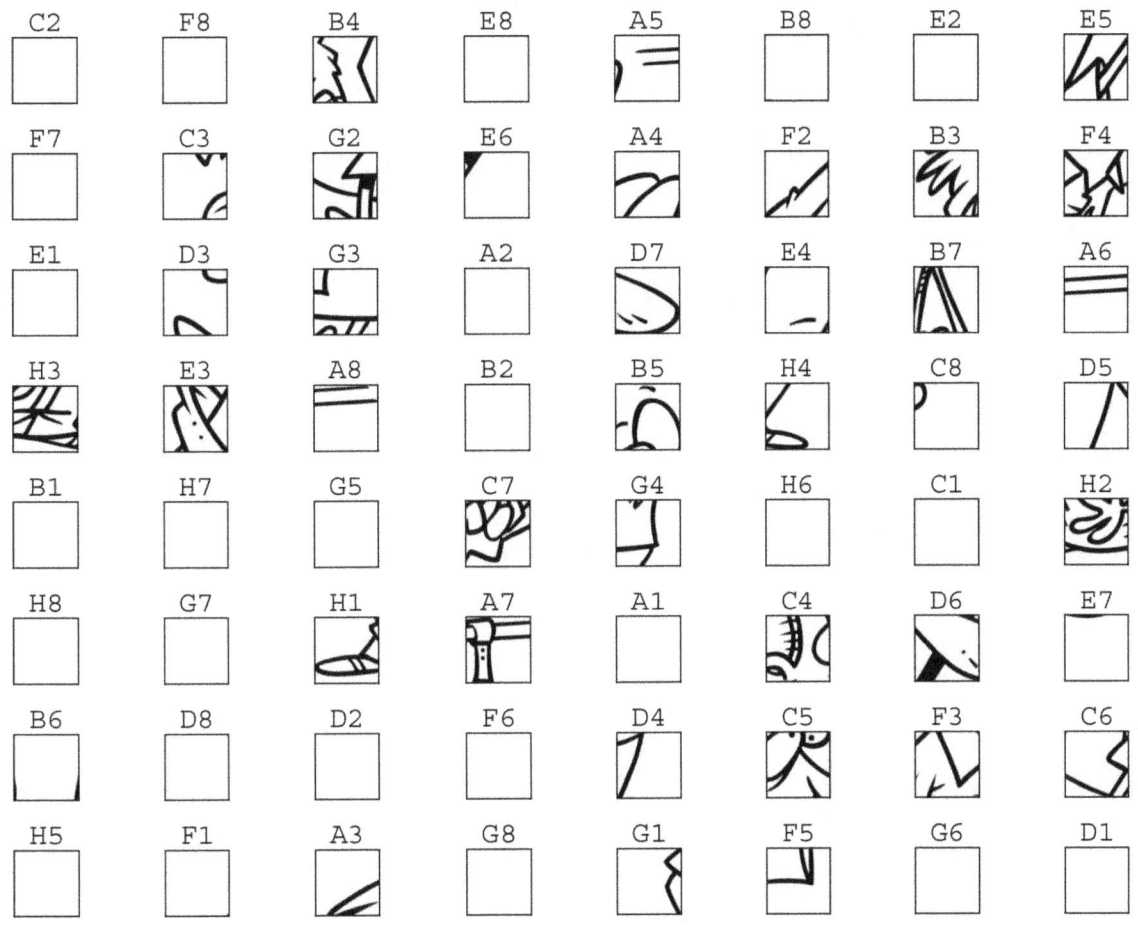
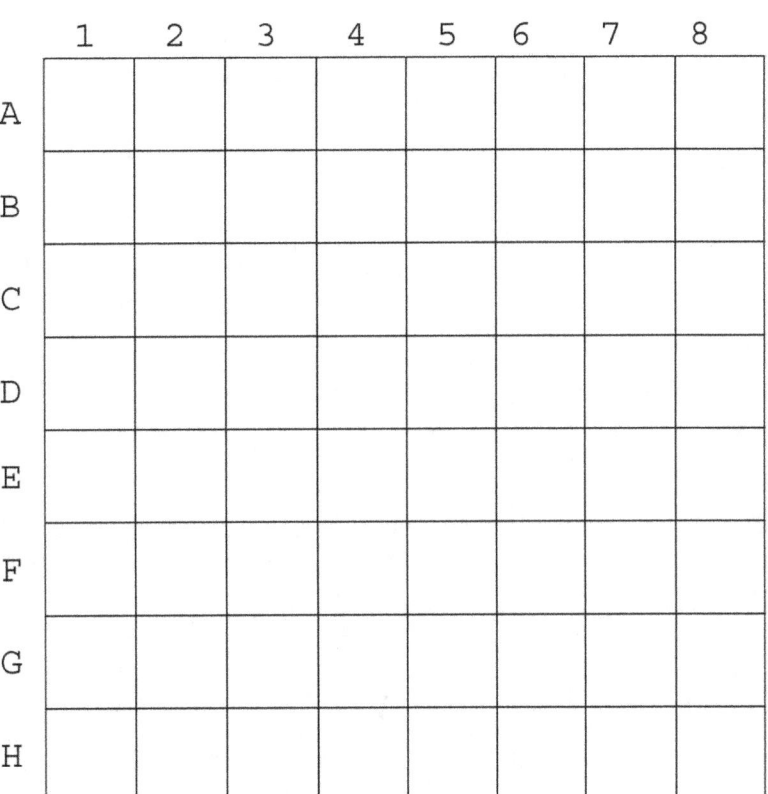

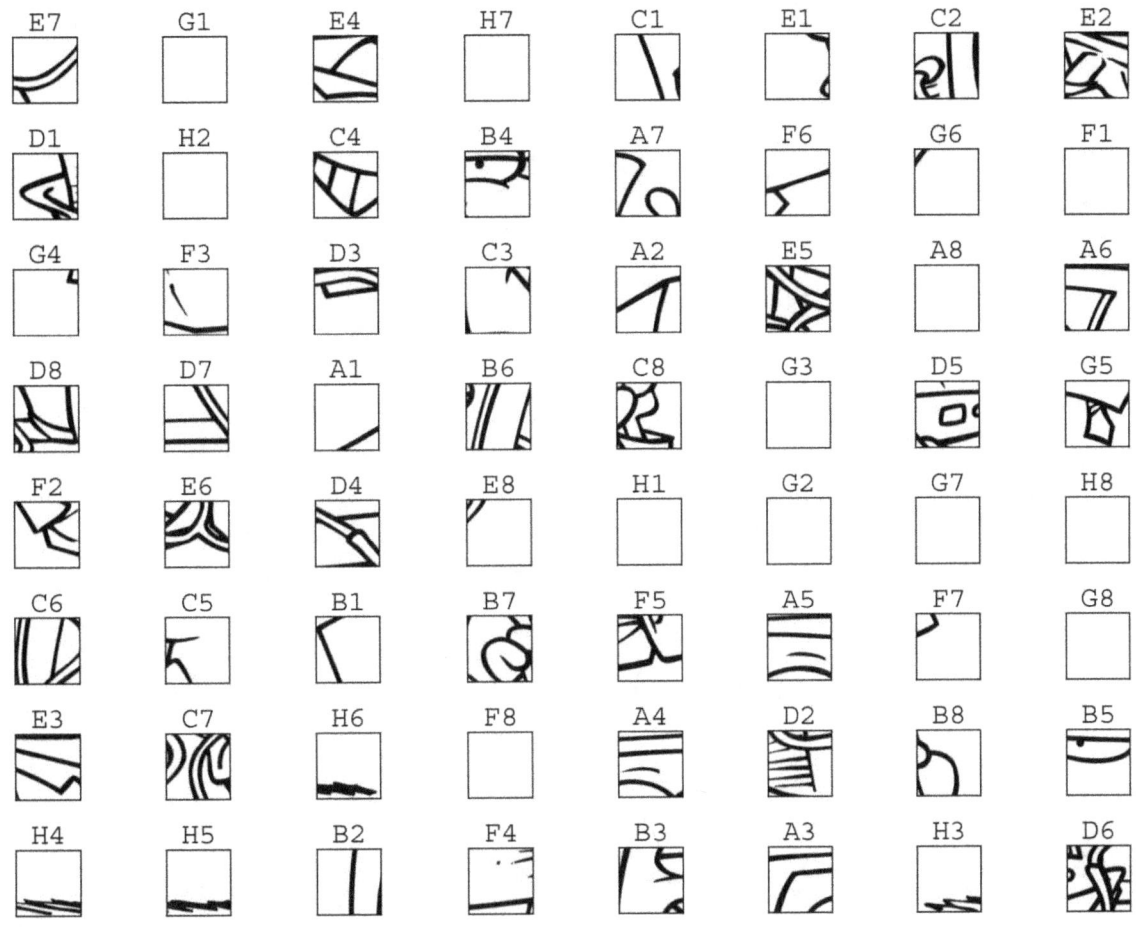
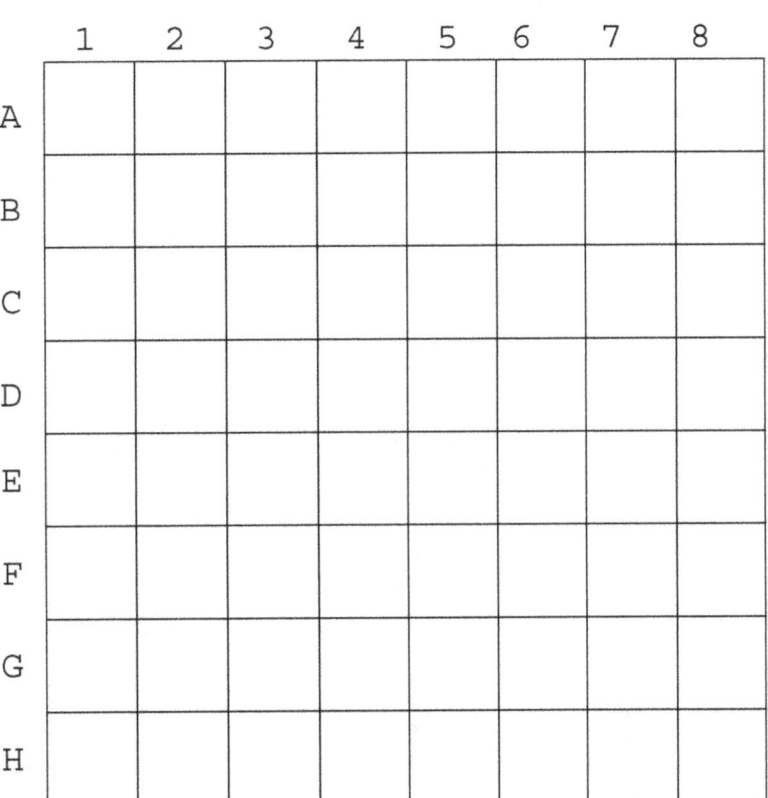

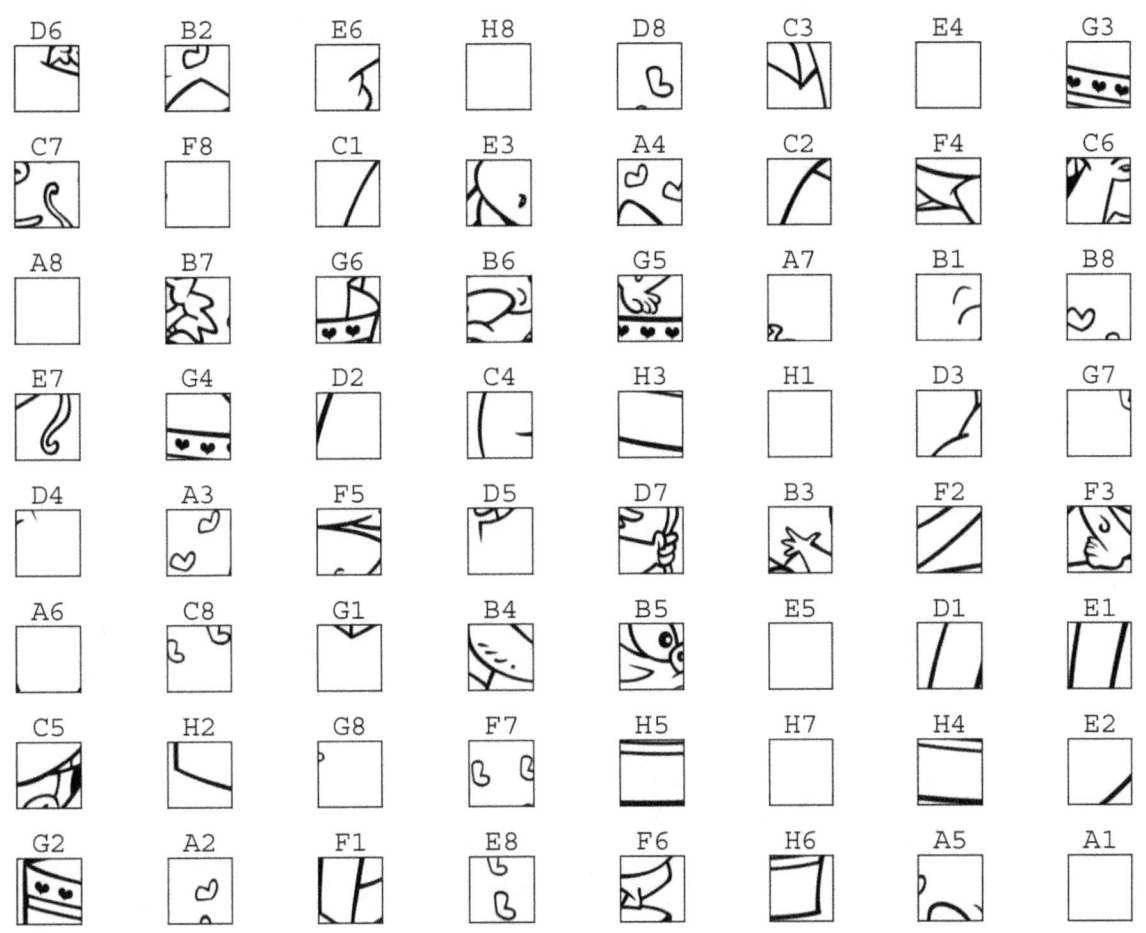
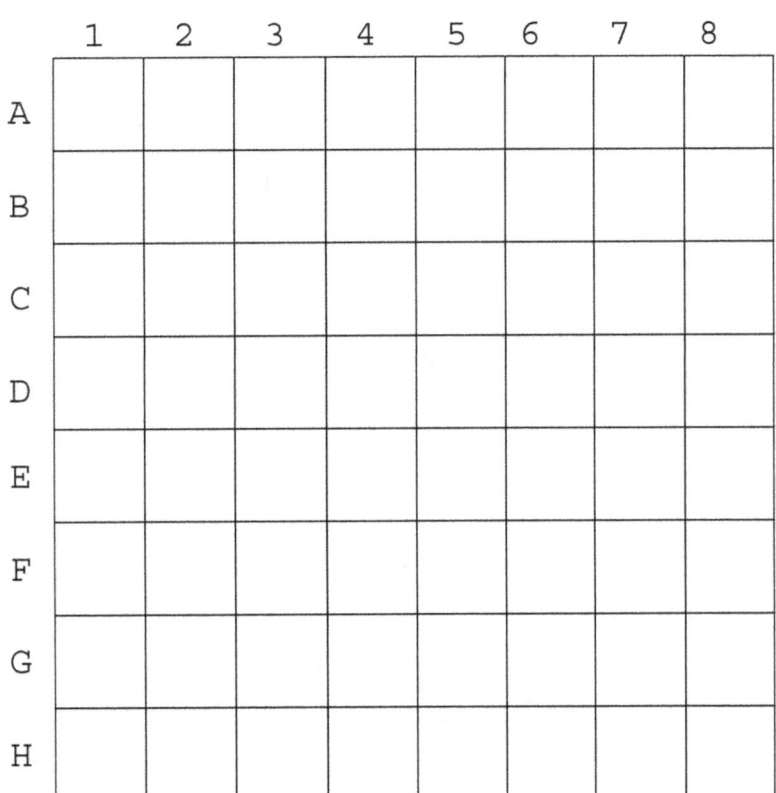

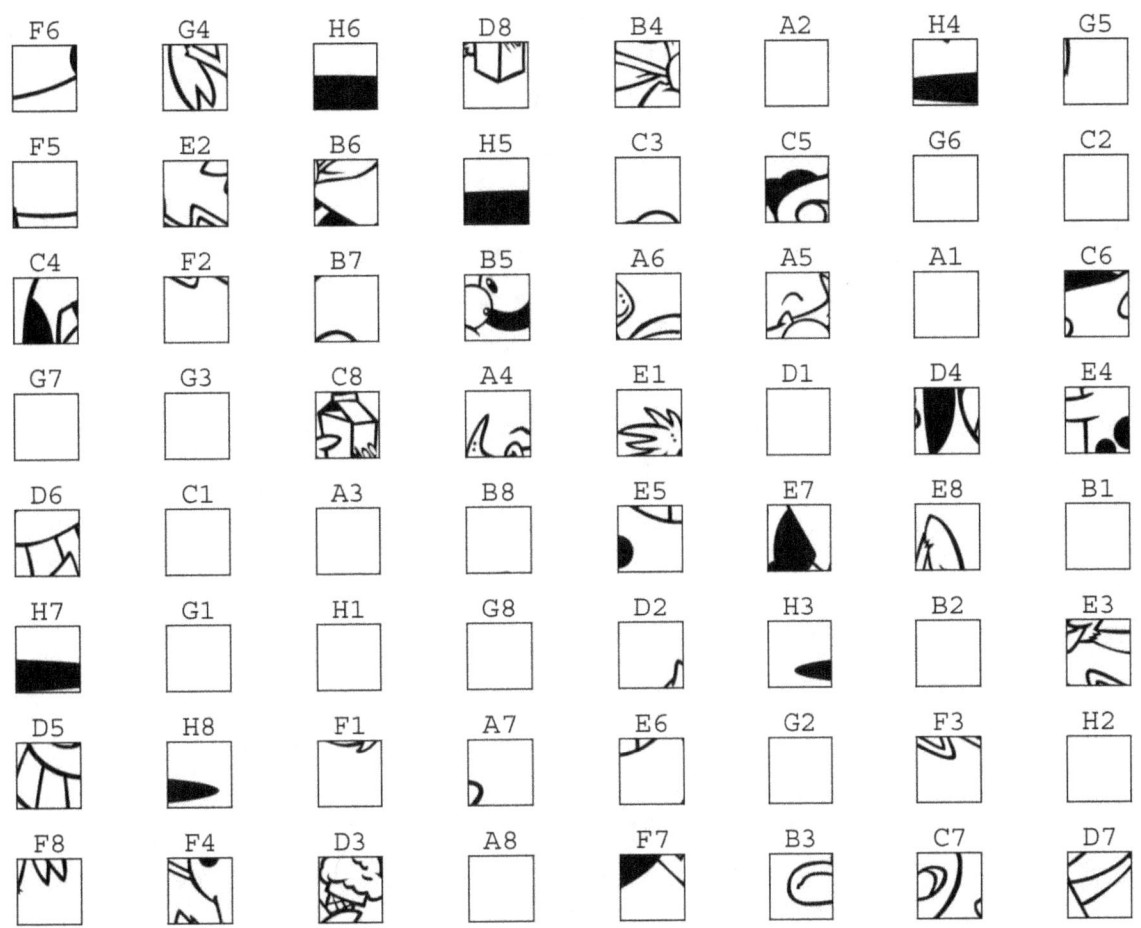
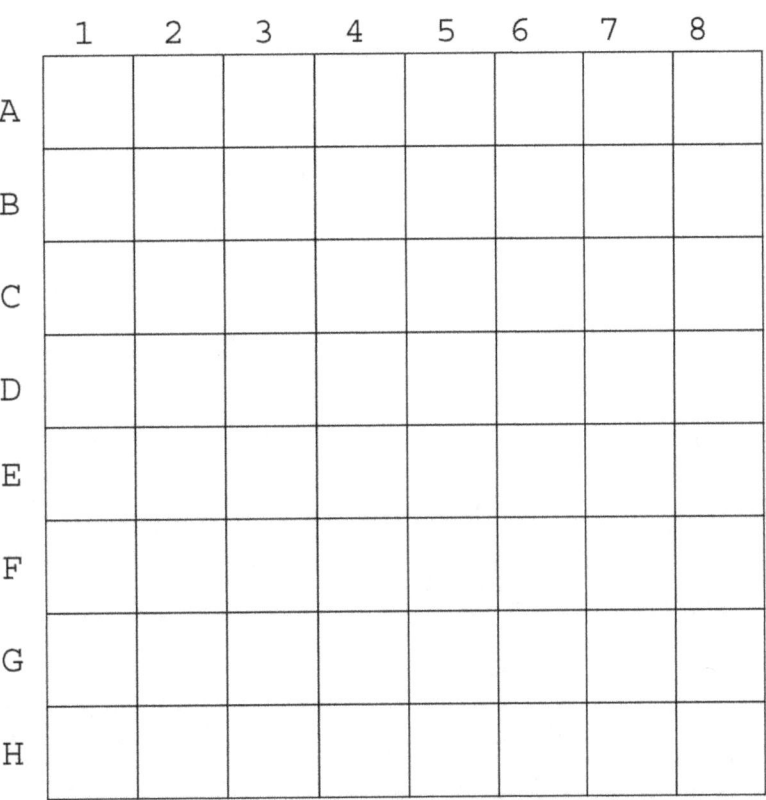

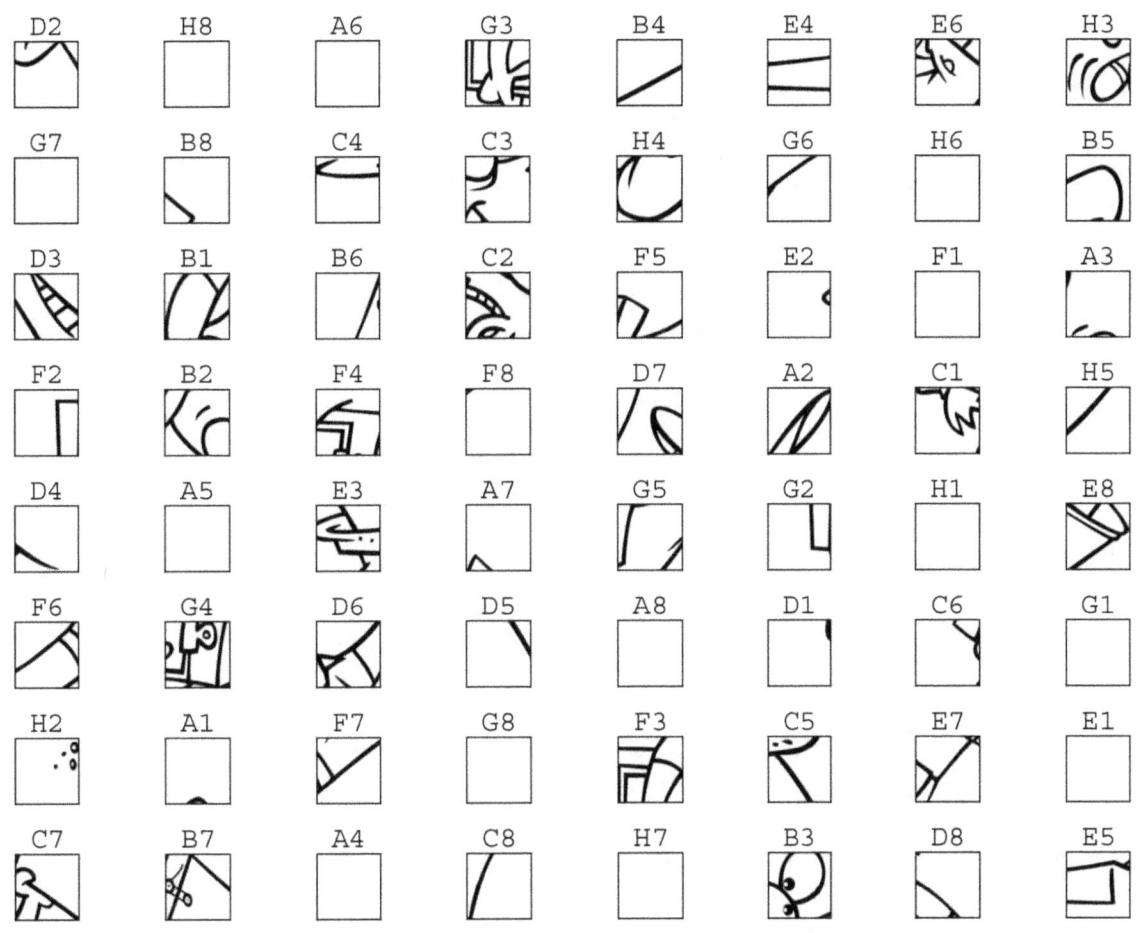
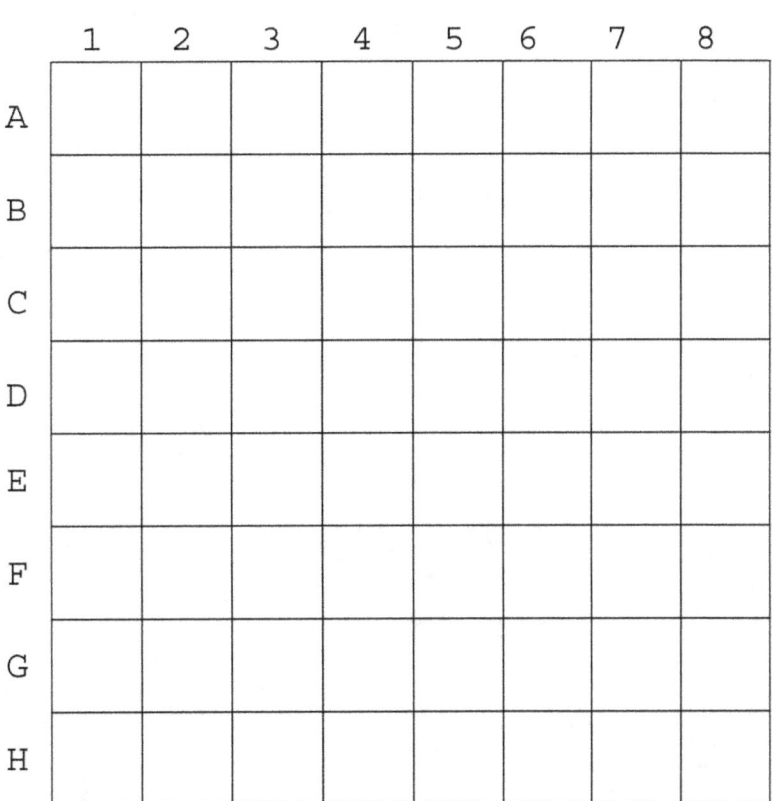

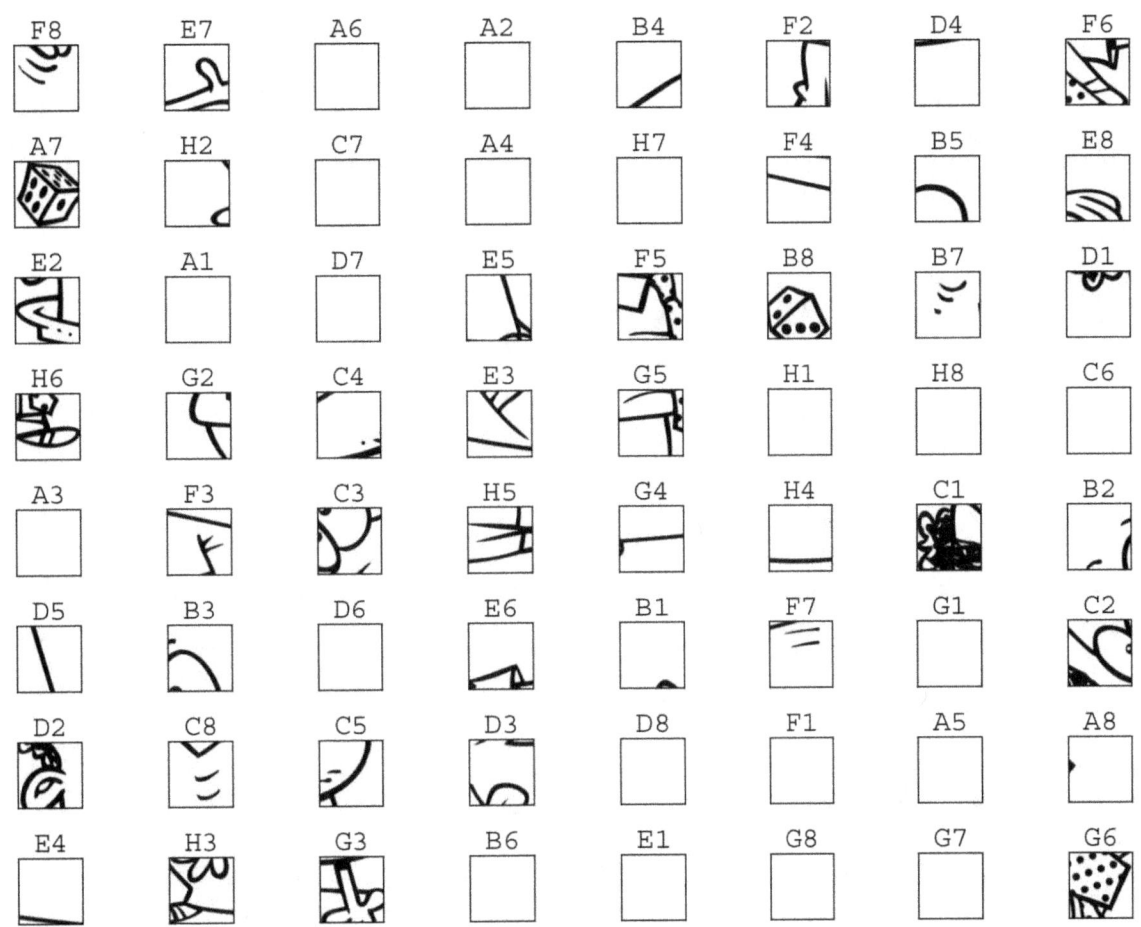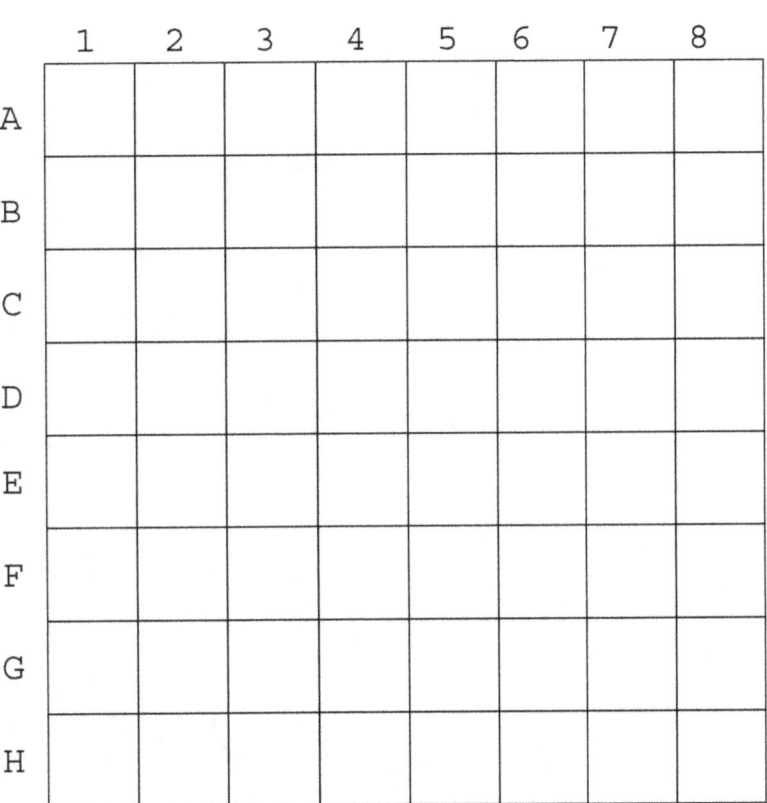

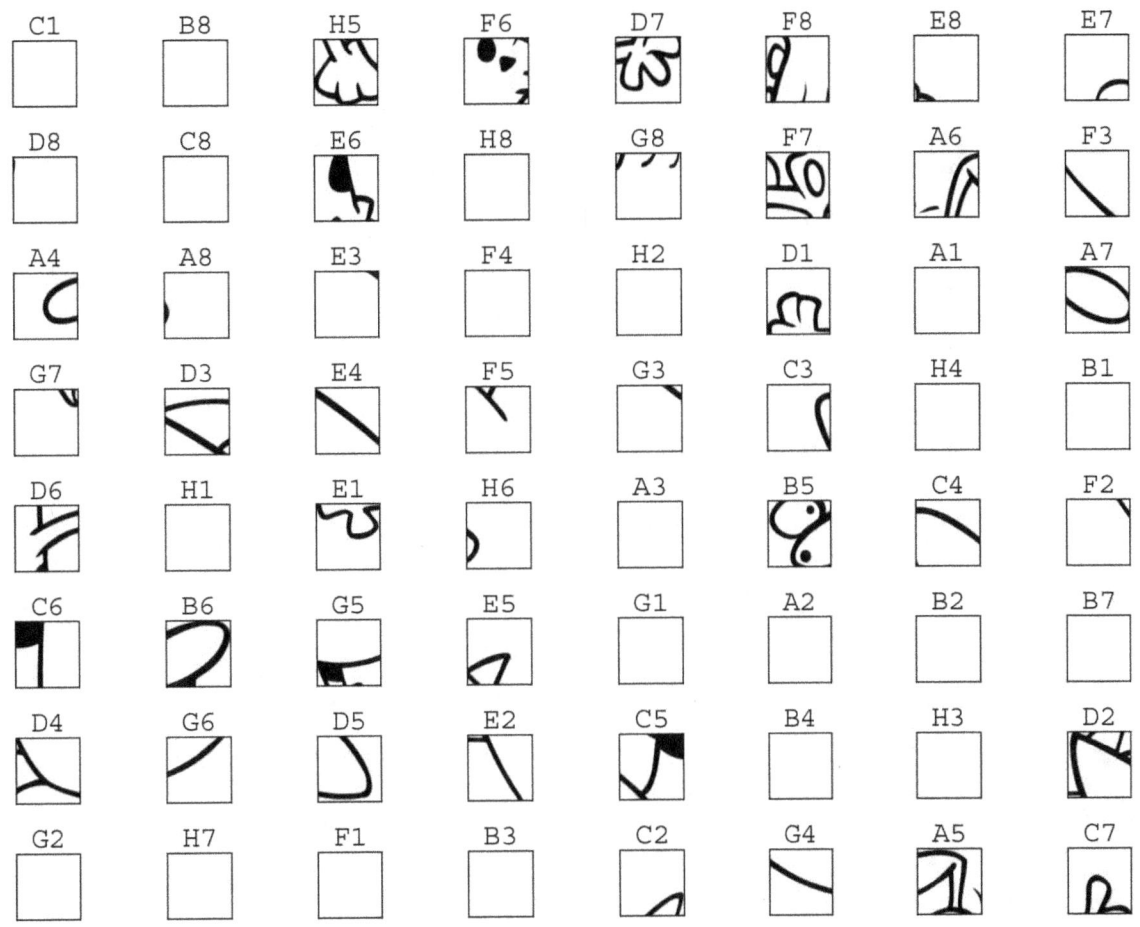
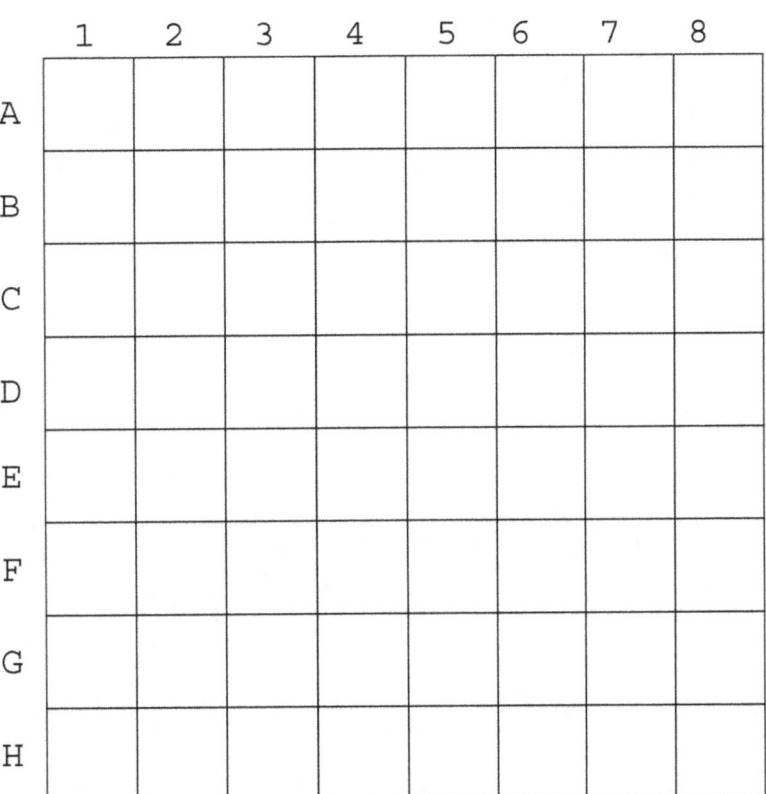

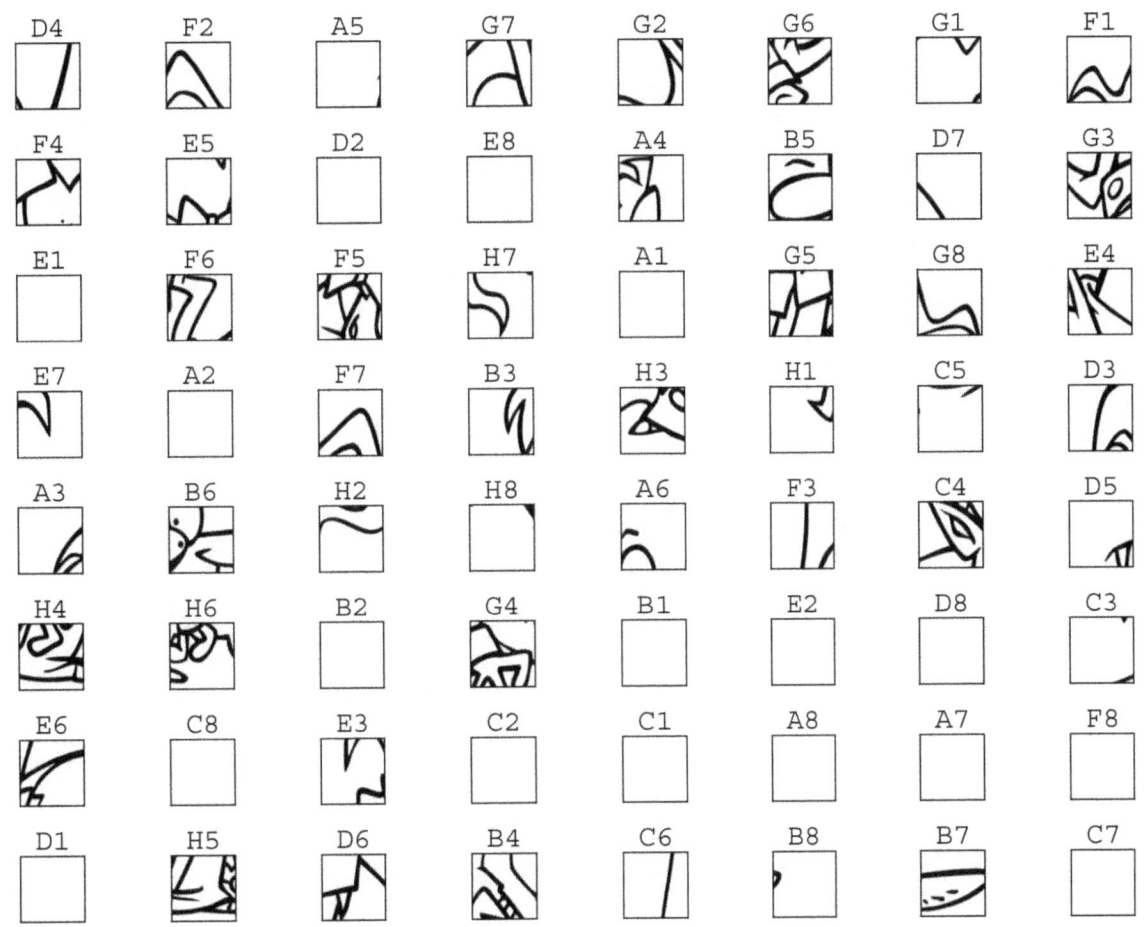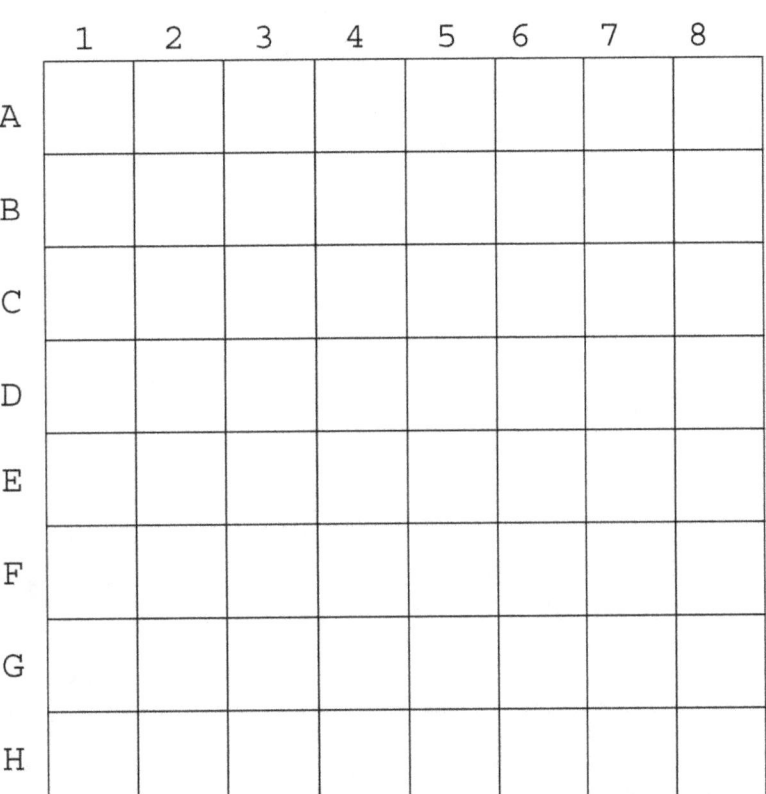

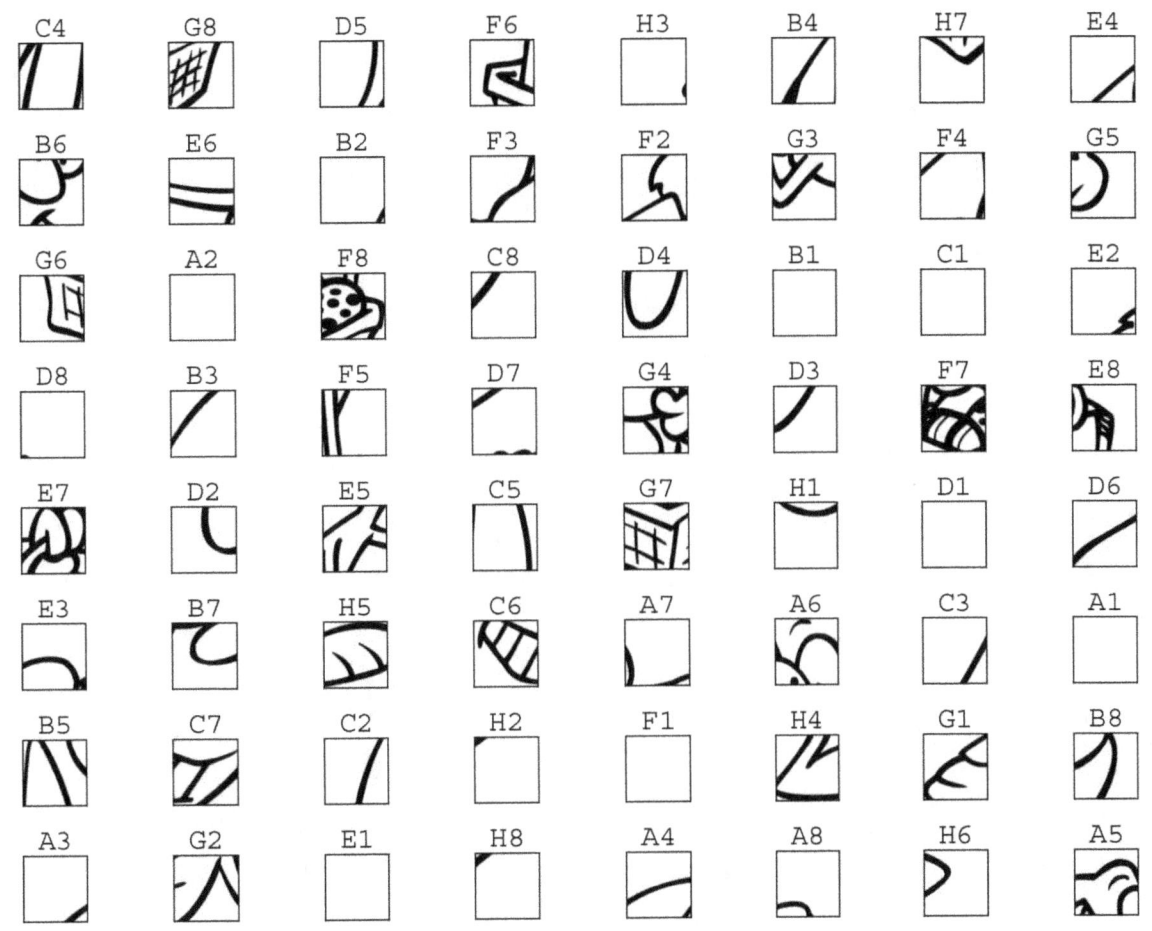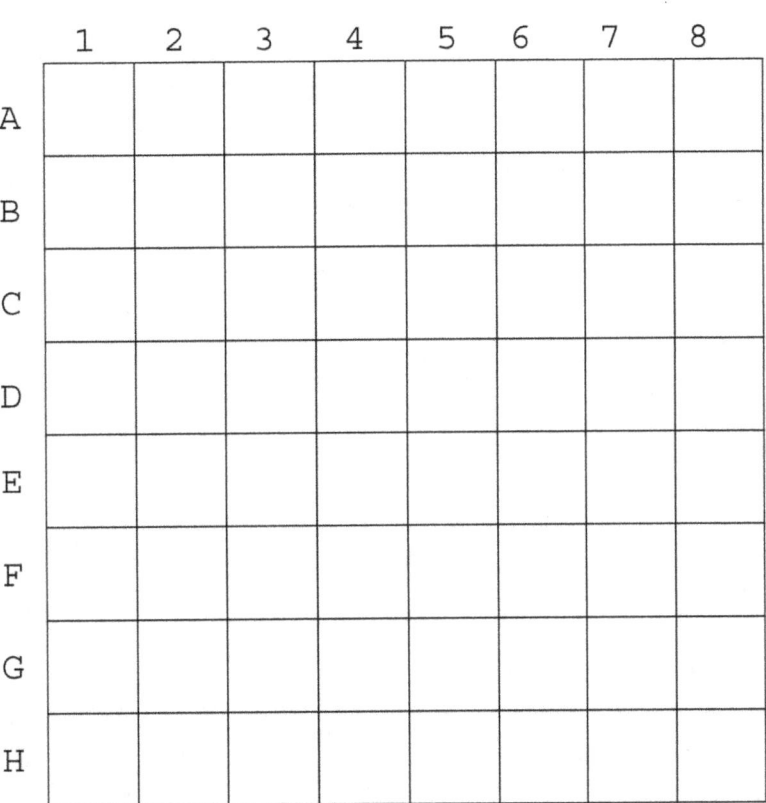

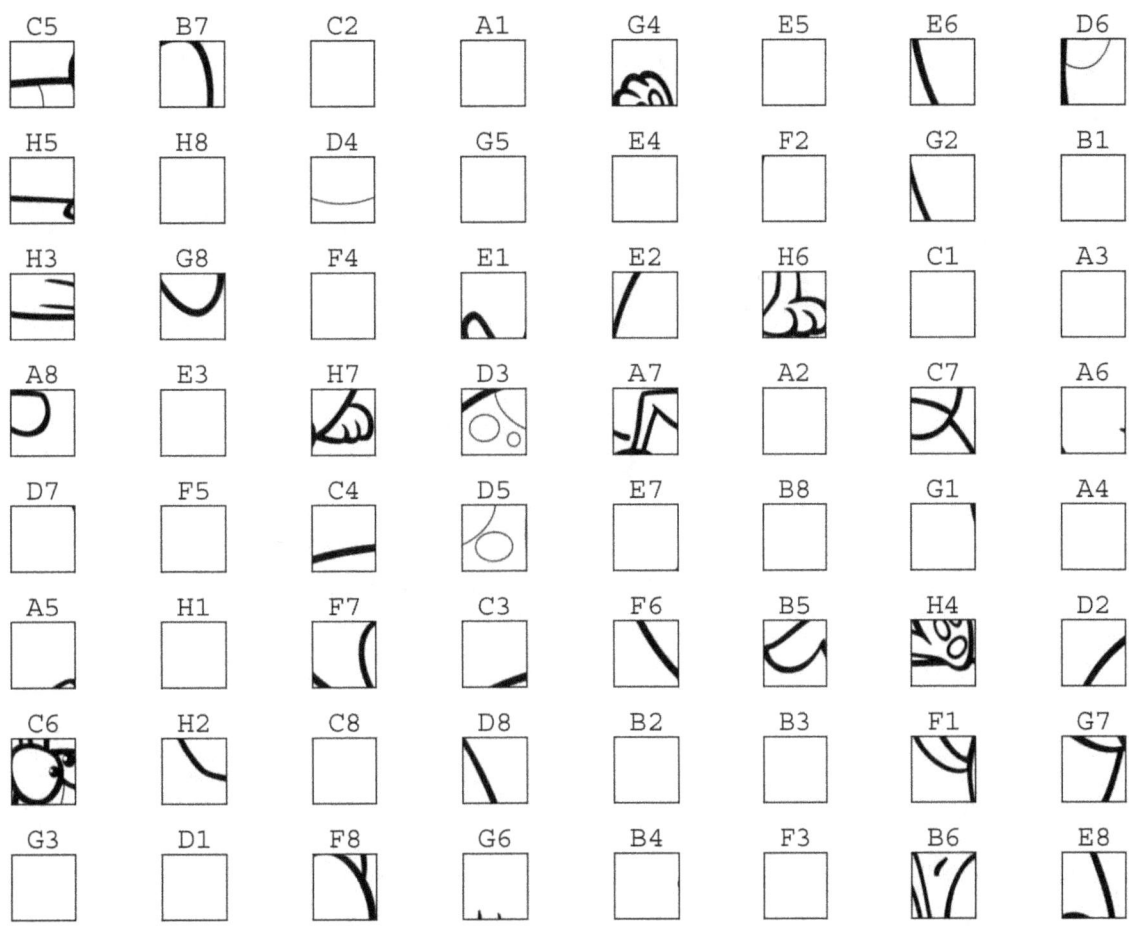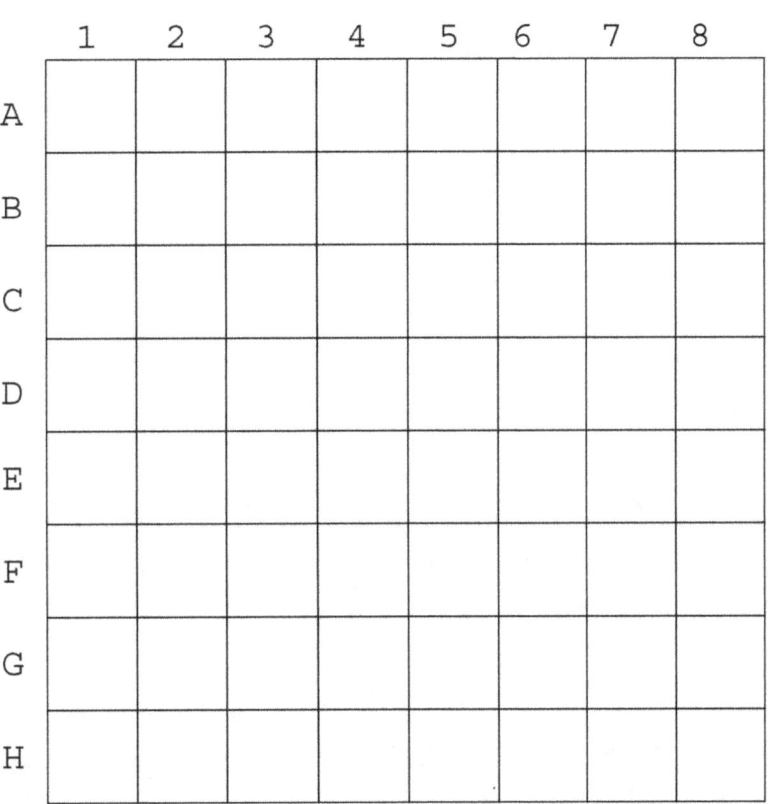

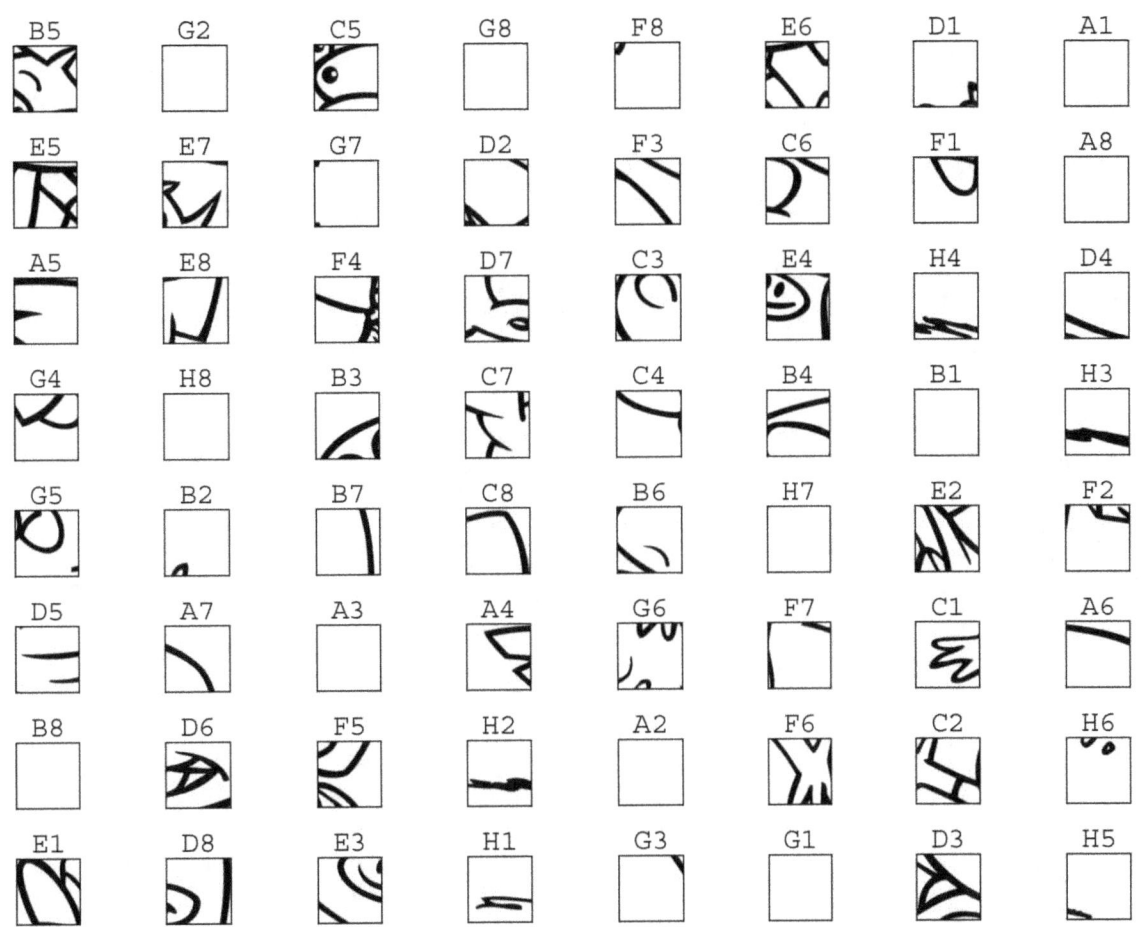
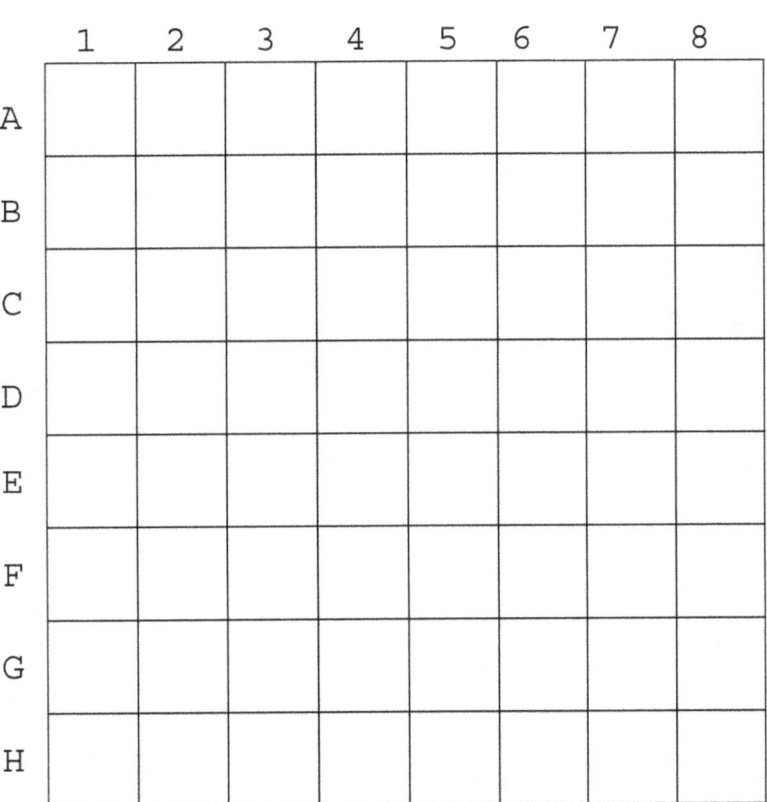

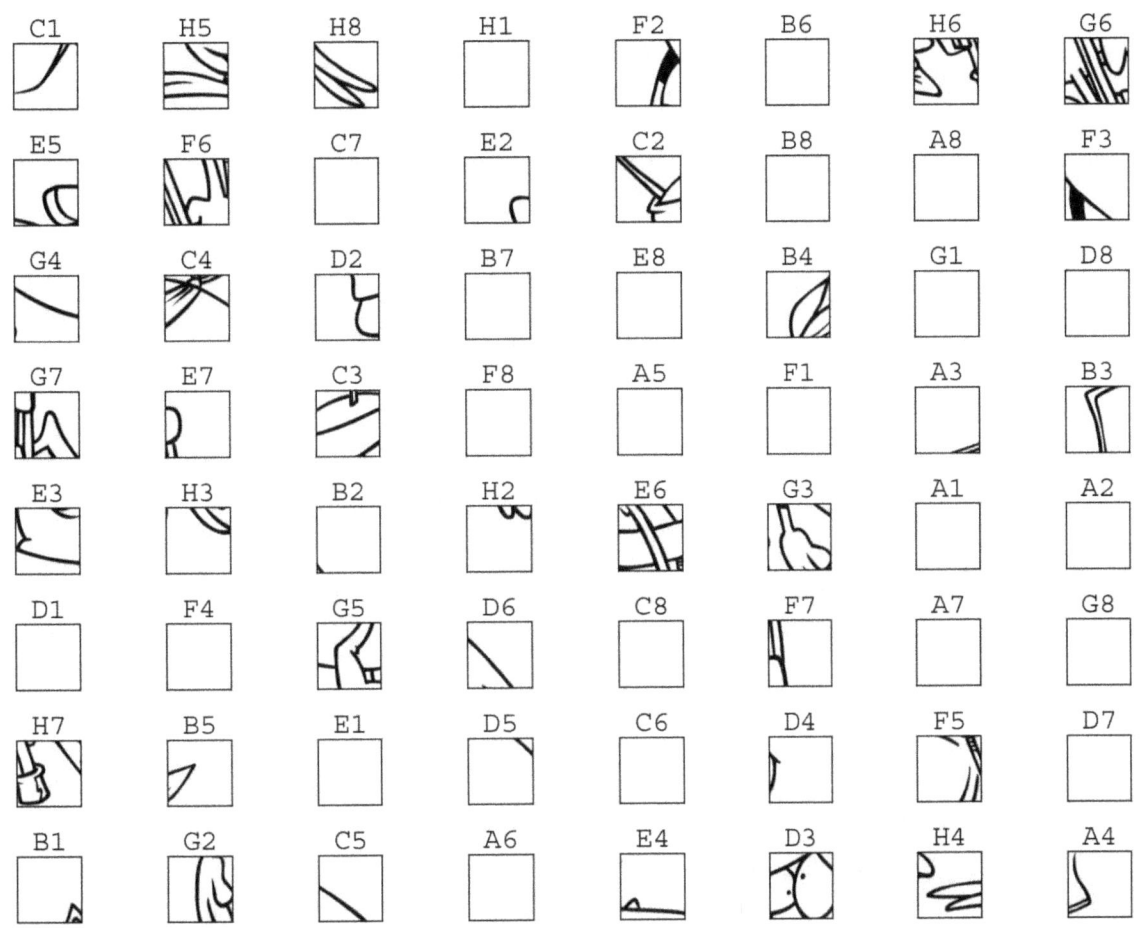
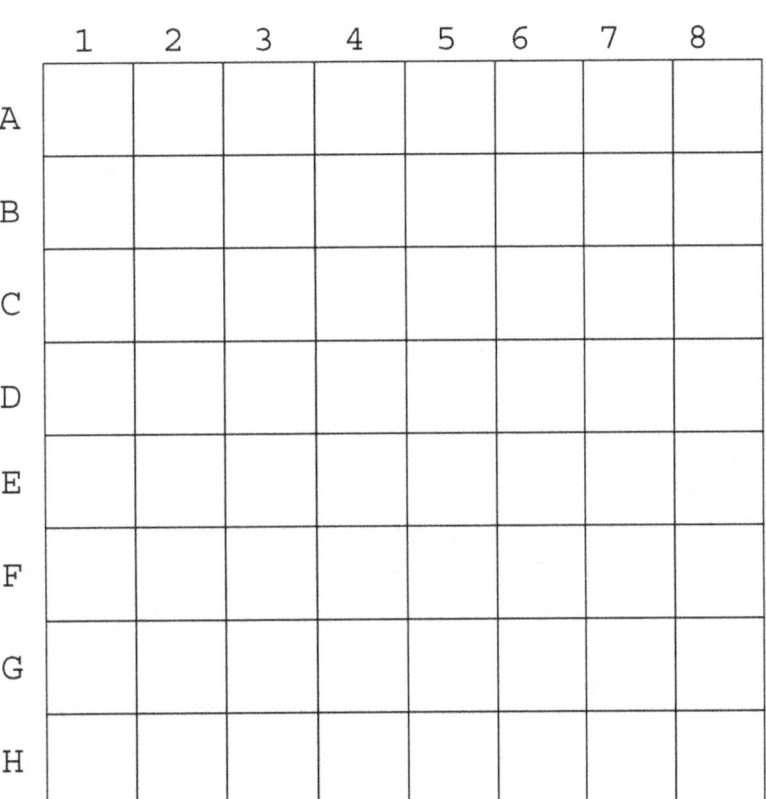

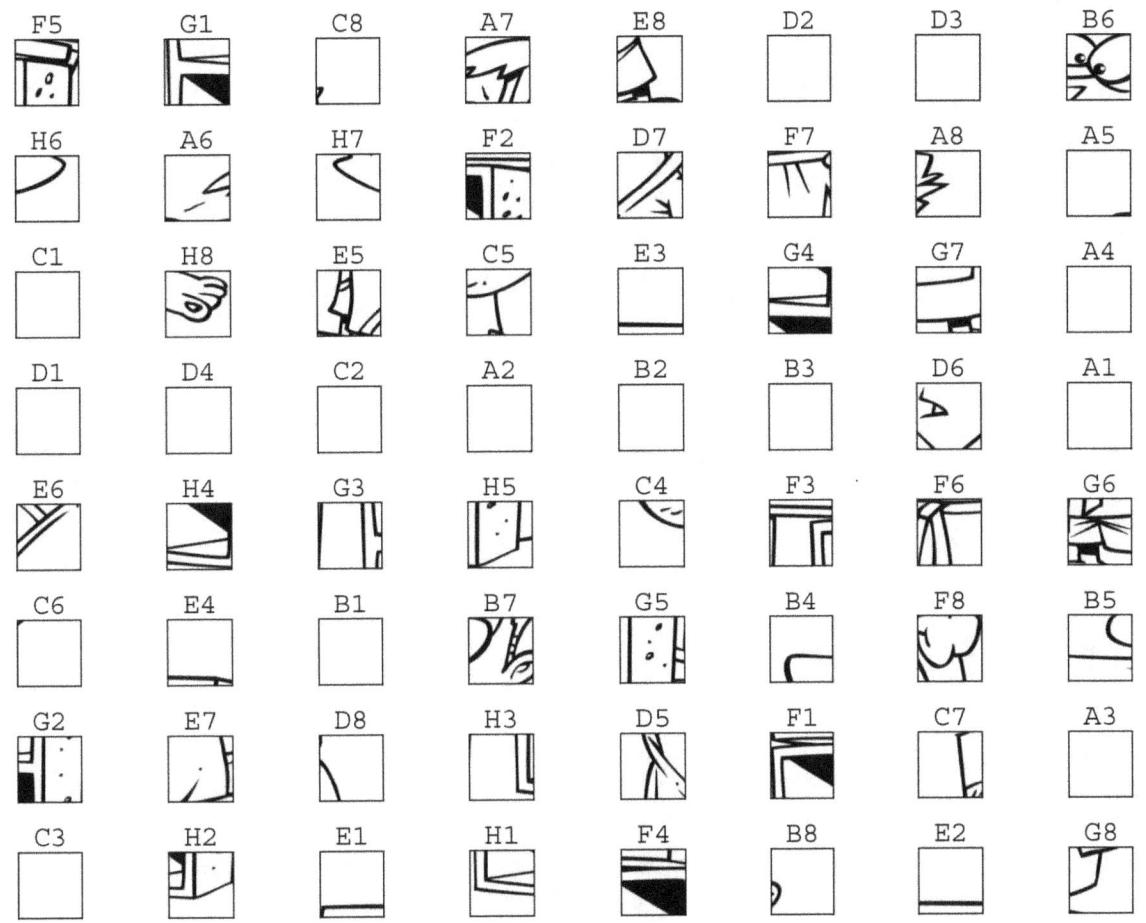
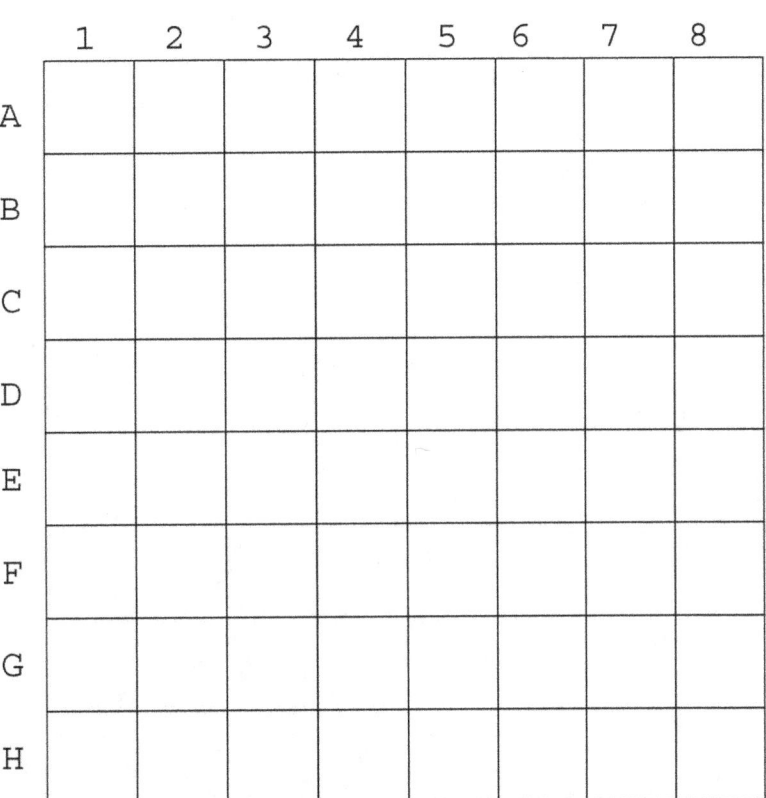

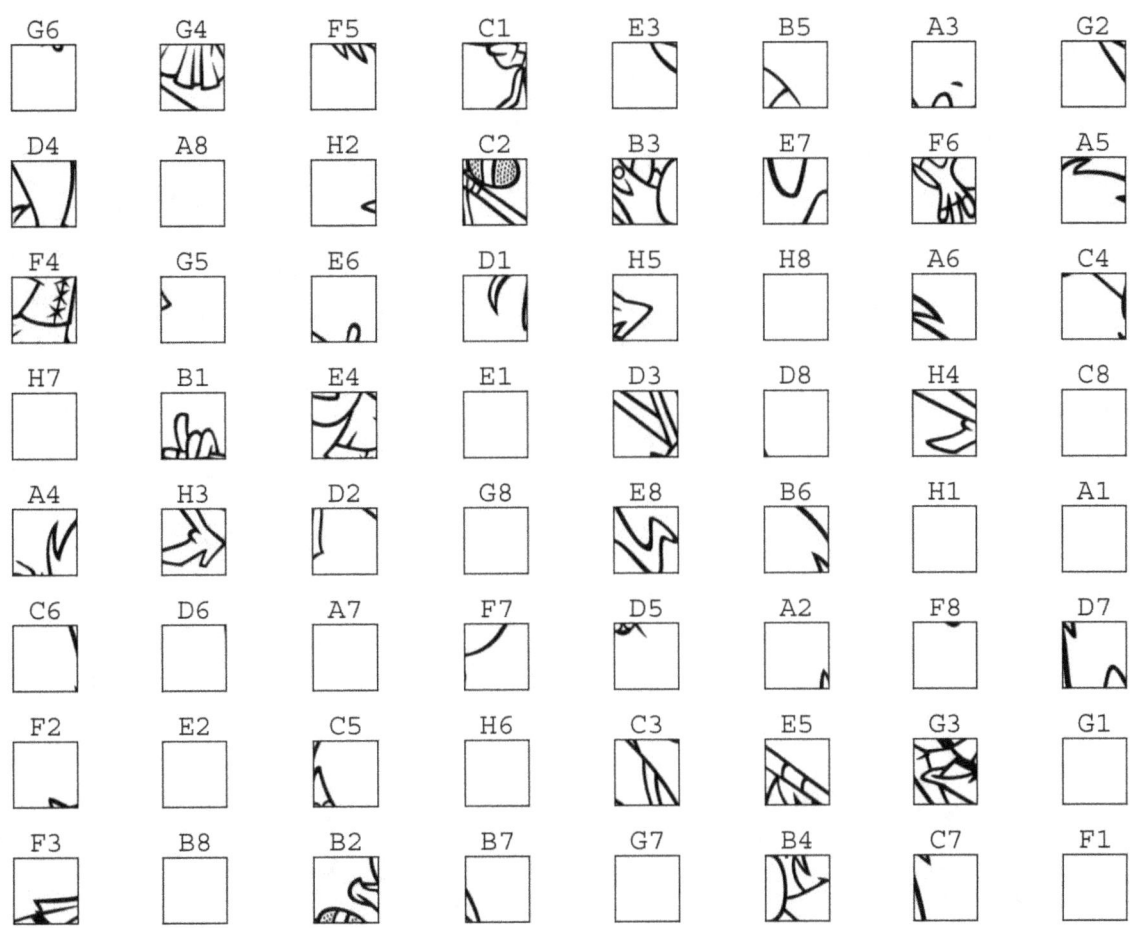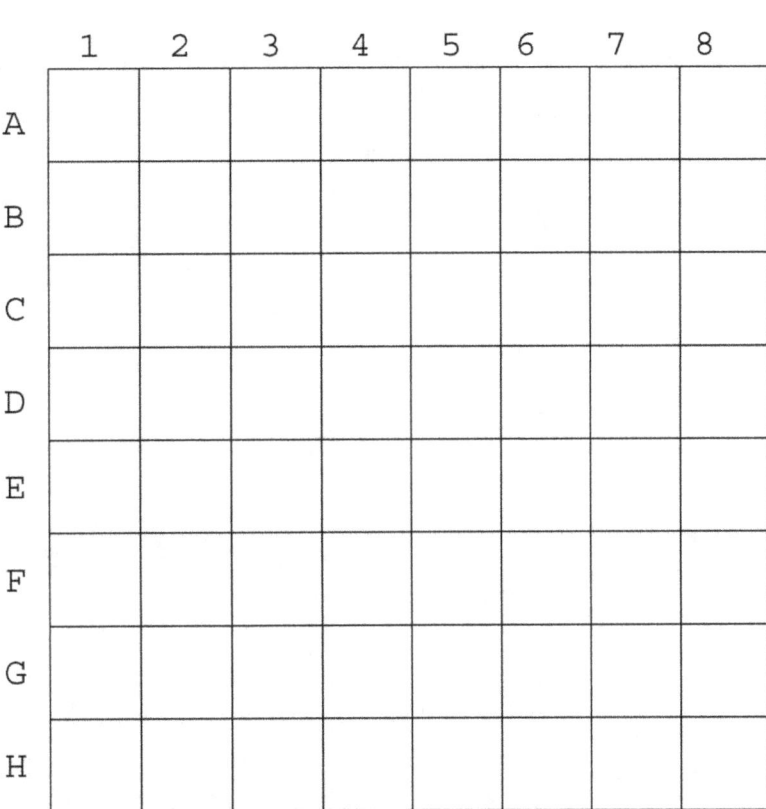

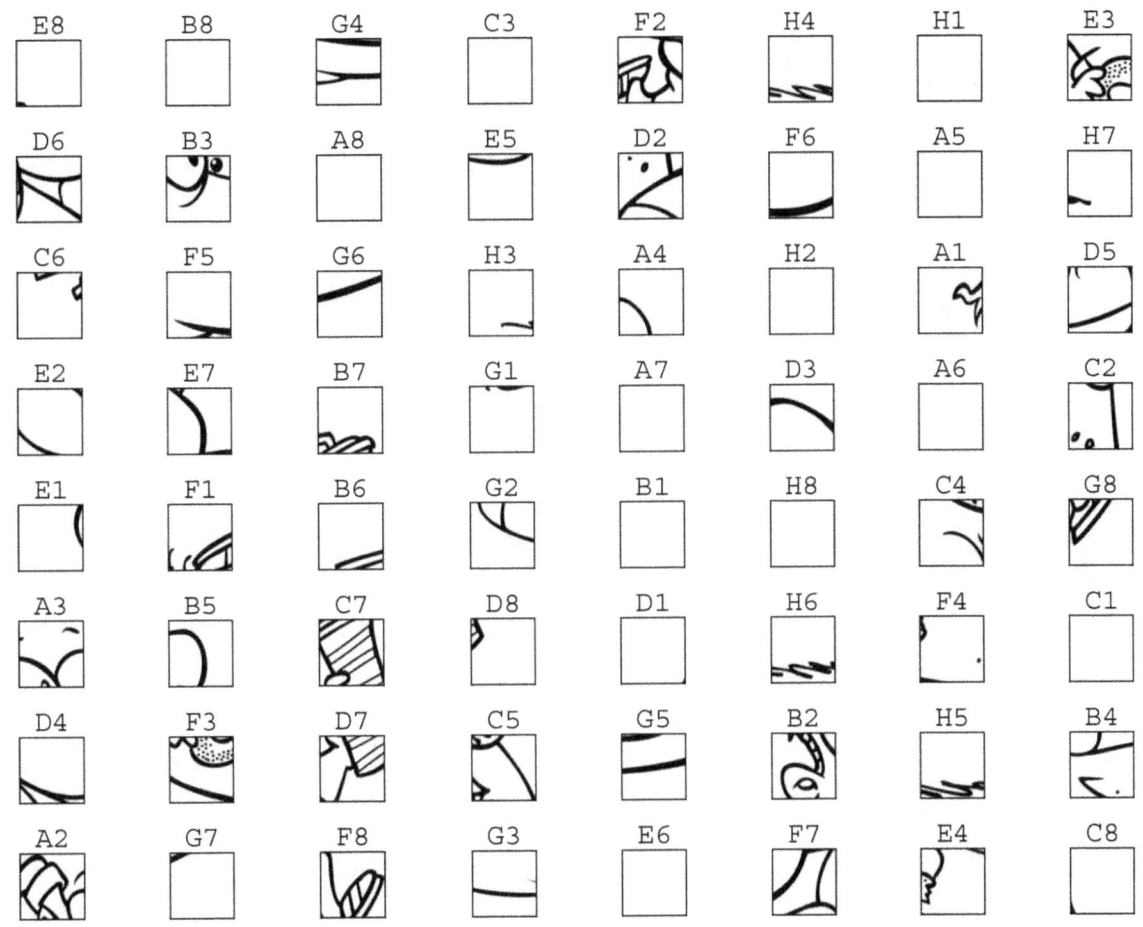
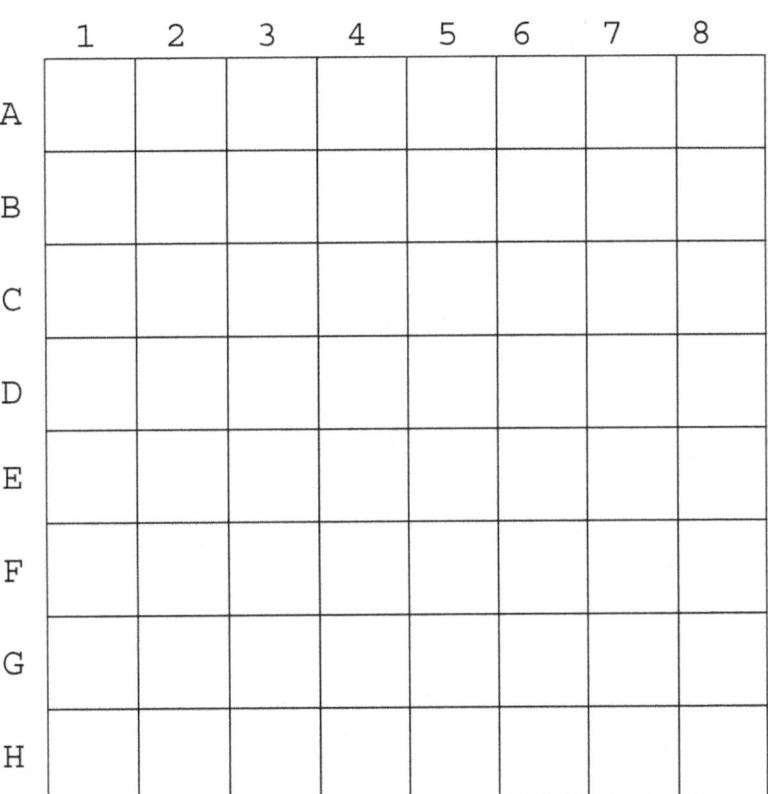

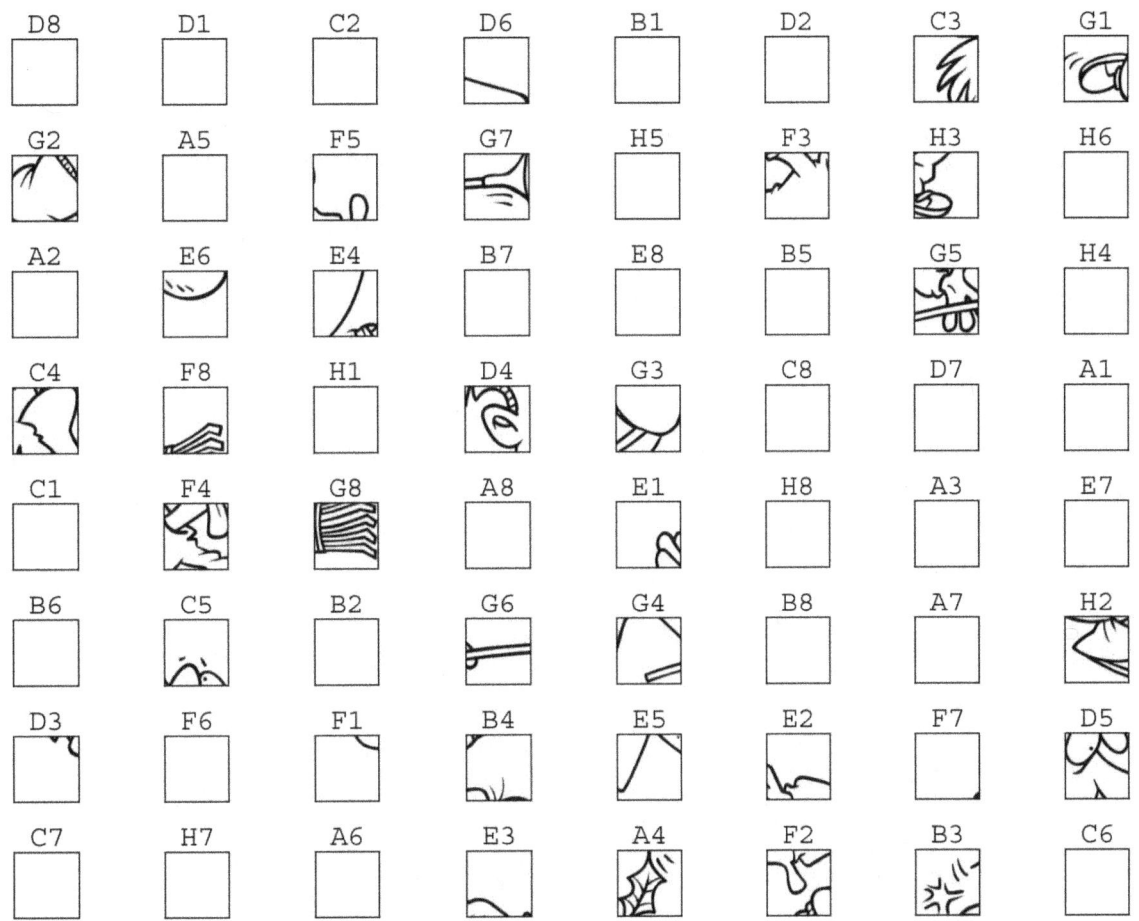
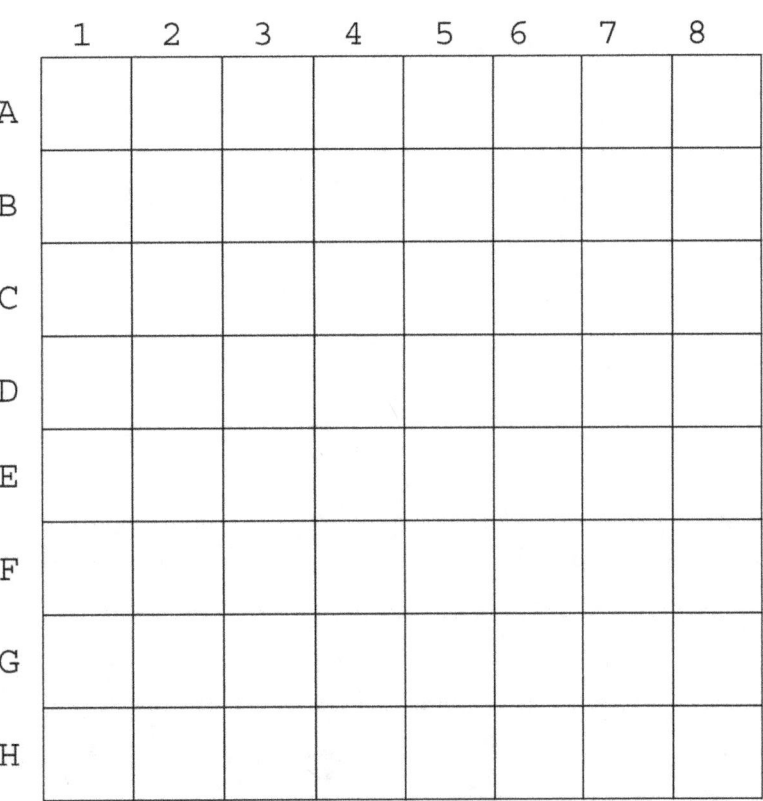

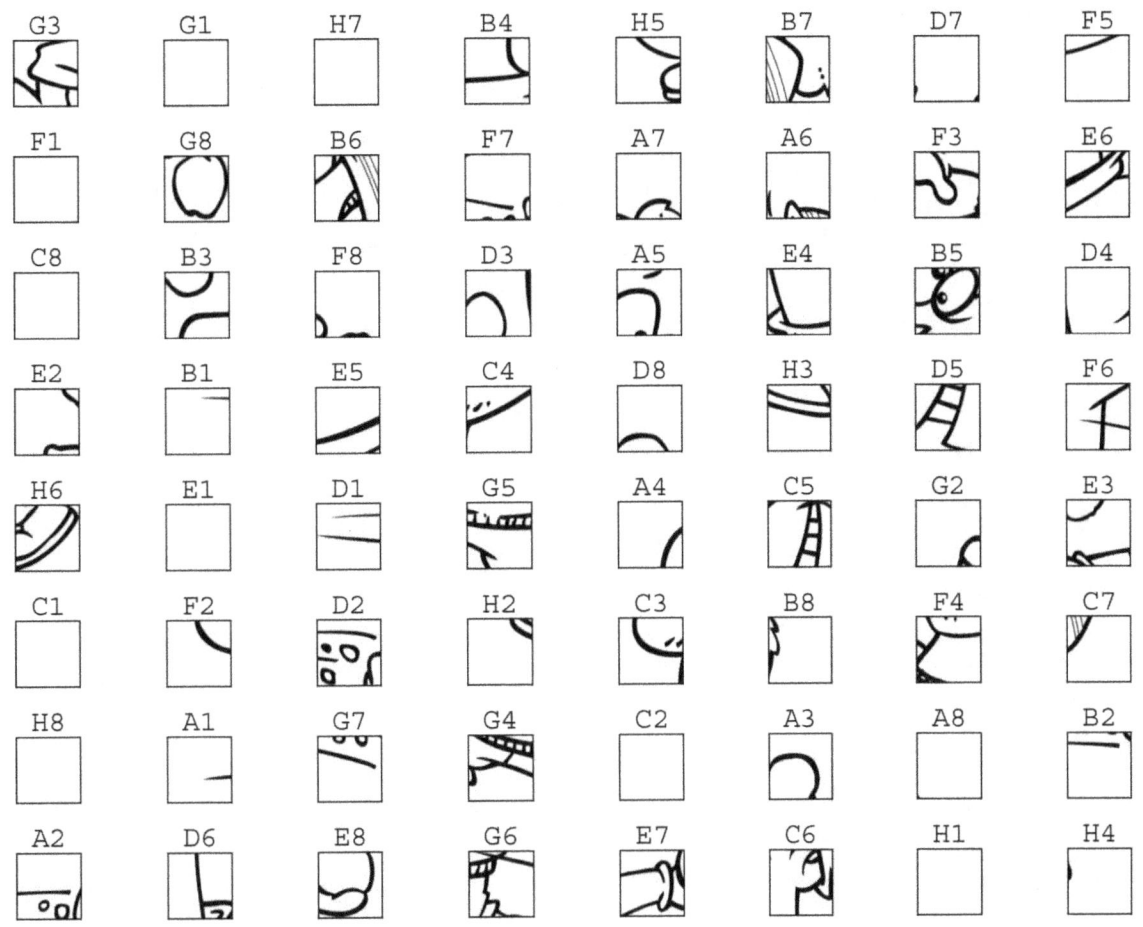
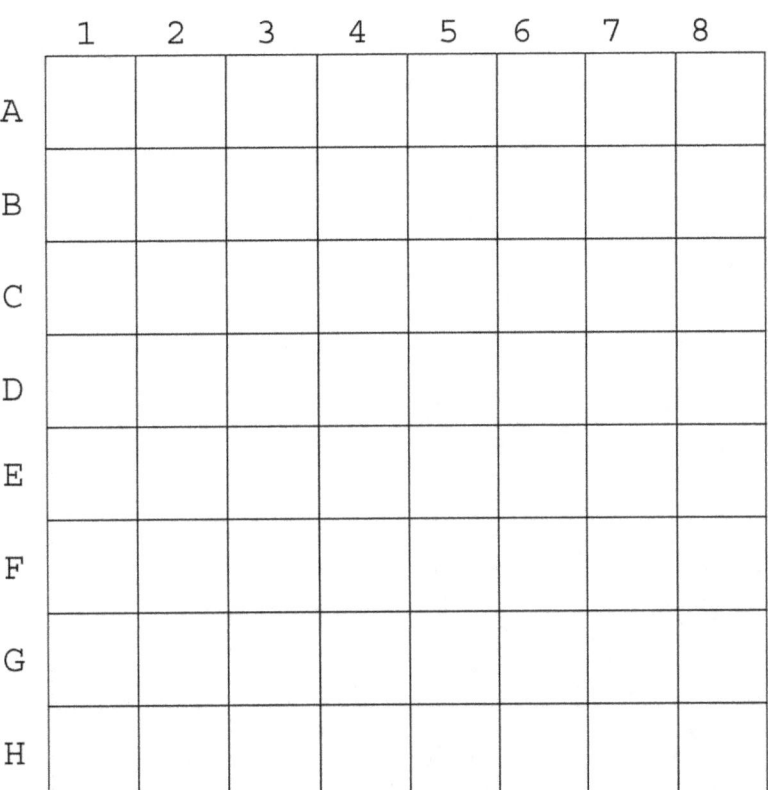

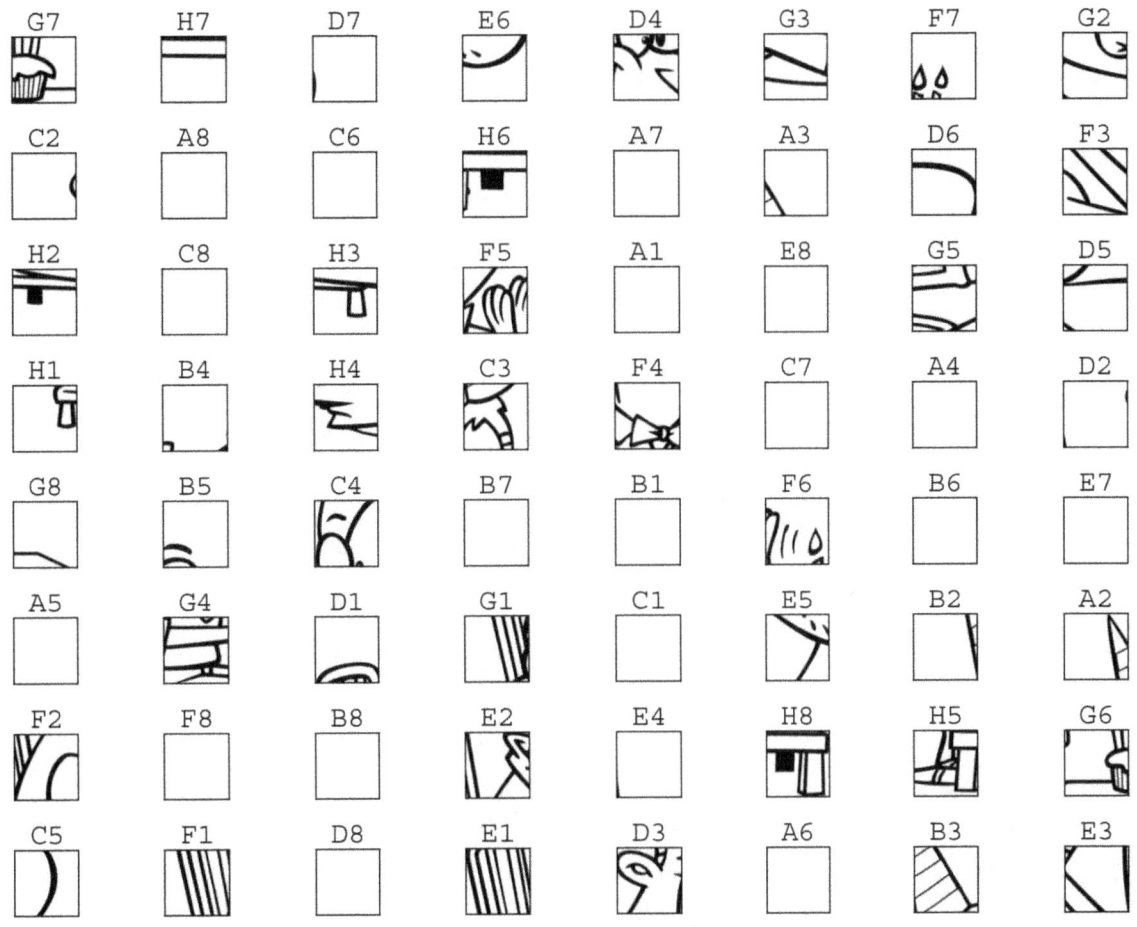
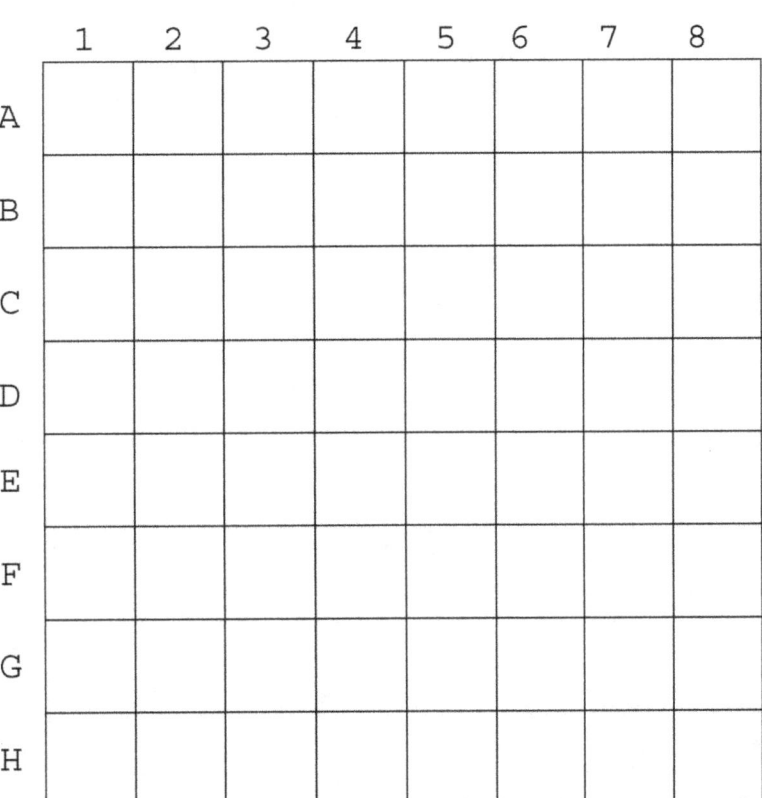

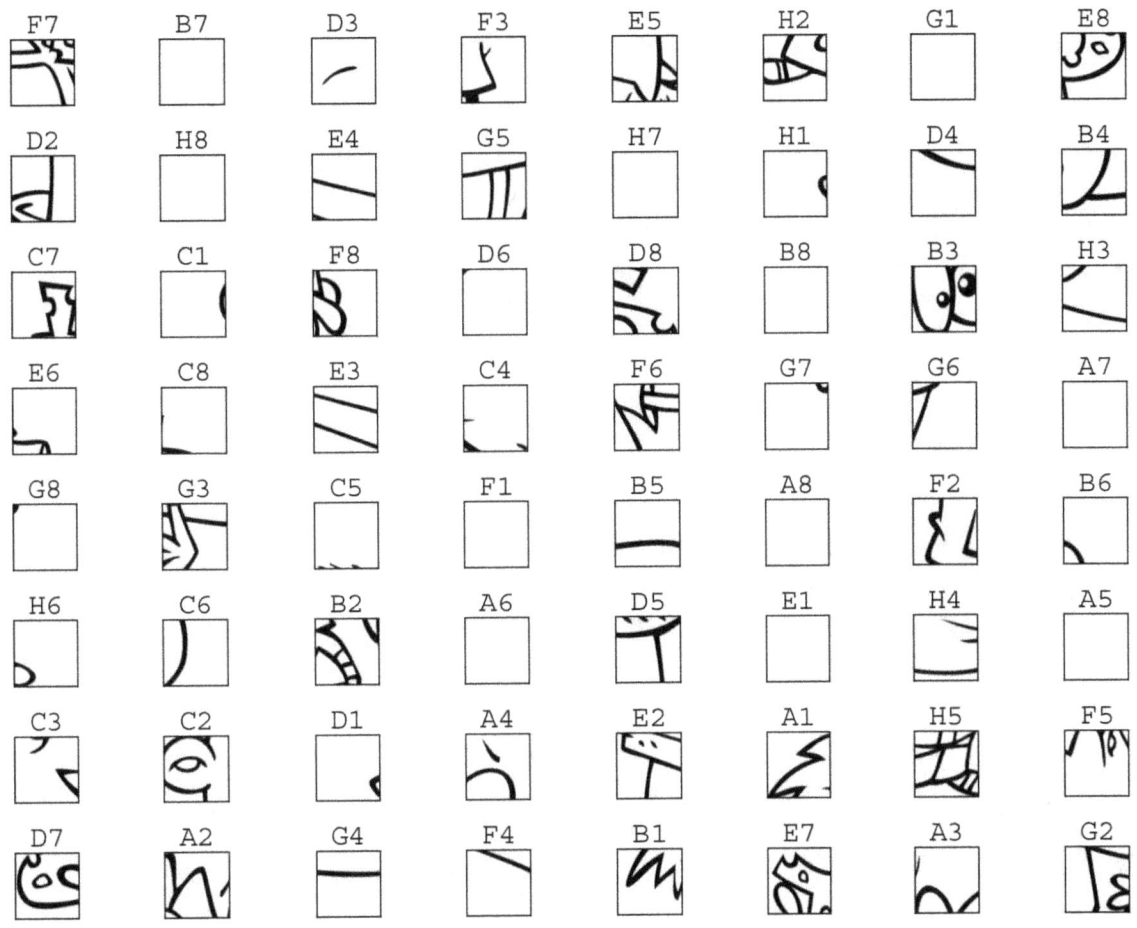
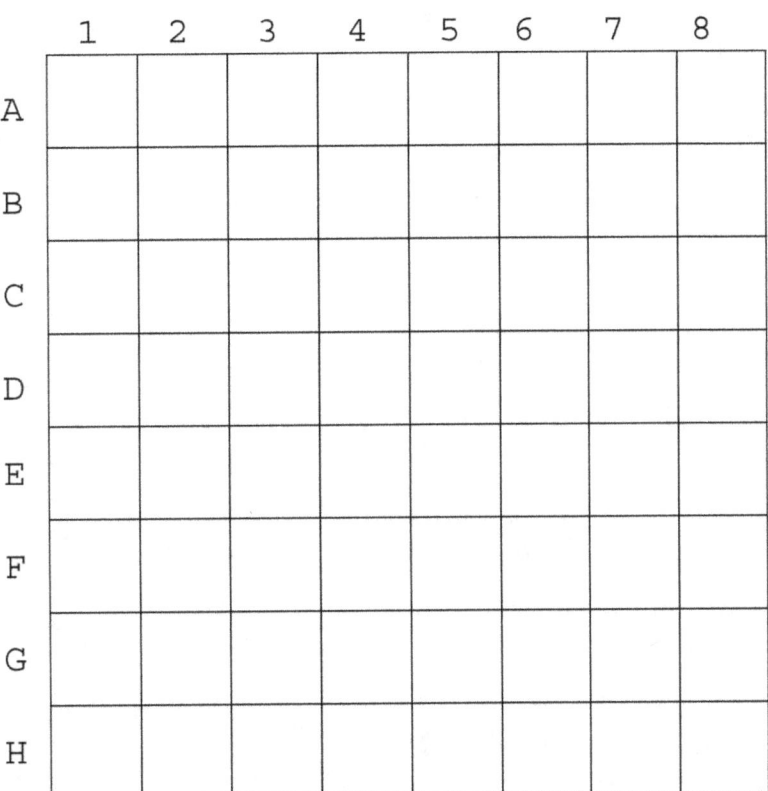

Thank you for completing our book! We appreciate your time and hope you enjoyed the experience. If you're up for more creative challenges, check out our other Pik-Jig books. Explore new grids and dive into the joy of artistic discovery. Happy drawing!

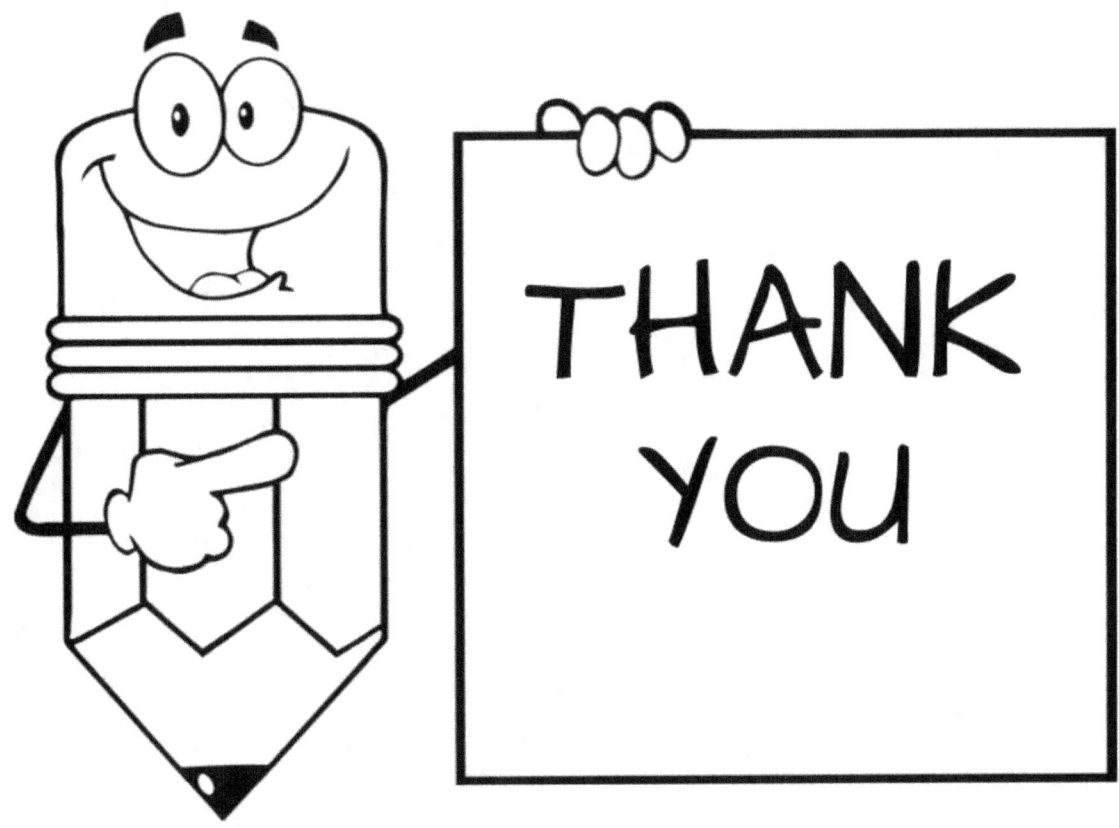

www.ingramcontent.com/pod-product-compliance
Lightning Source LLC
Chambersburg PA
CBHW062120220526
45471CB00010B/3810